Joining God's Army

Autobiography of a Soldier

Lester K. Anderson

Published by AKA:yola / AKA-Publishing
Columbia, Missouri
www.akayola.com

Library of Congress
Anderson, Lester K.
Joining God's Army: Autobiography of a Soldier

1. Salvation Army 2. Humanitarian
3. Christianity   4. Panama 5. Autobiography

ISBN: 978-1-936688-01-2

AKA-Publishing
AKA:yola

www.AKA-Publishing.com
www.AKAyola.com

Introduction

BETWEEN A ROCK AND A HARD PLACE

This painting is from a 1934 black and white photograph taken of our family when we lived on a farm close to Eldridge, North Dakota. After three years of crop failure, without funds to pay the rent, we were evicted from our farm. While my father Victor was away, men came and removed all our furniture and possessions from our house to the other side of the road. They then locked the door. We were told that our mother Clara was baking bread in our cookstove which the men removed by putting boards under it. We are seen here waiting for friends to take us to Jamestown. My stories begin the day of this picture.

A local photographer came out the eleven miles from town and shot this picture of our sad looking family, another family who were victims of the depression. Our mother was so embarrassed that she destroyed her copy of this picture. Many years later a copy was found among her sister Selma's belongings and I painted it on canvas with oil.

You can see the original painting at Frontier Village in Jamestown, North Dakota, at the Eldridge General Store and Post office which was where my father and Wayne rode horseback to pick up the mail.

The painting is from left to right: Victor, Wayne, Clara and Lester. There were three other children: Leonard, Blanche and Gladys who had moved to town. Our sister Vivian was deceased.

TABLE OF CONTENTS

Three Gates

If you are tempted to reveal
A tale to you someone has told
About another, make it pass,
Before you speak, three gates of gold.
These narrow gates:
First, "Is it true?"
Then, "Is it needful?"
In your mind give truthful answer.
And the next is last and narrowest,
"Is it kind?"
And if to reach your lips at last
It passes through these gateways three,
Then you may tell the tale, nor fear
What the result of speech may be.

FROM THE ARABIAN

CHAPTER ONE

MEMORABLE MOMENTS

Moving to Town

We lost our farm by Eldridge, North Dakota, in the fall of 1934 when I was two years old. My father known as Vic and my mother as Clara, Wayne, my older brother by two and a half years, and I arrived at a small hotel in Jamestown on a cold November day.   I knew it was early winter because we were all wearing coats and hats.

I remember climbing the stairs to the hotel where we were to spend our first night in town. The door was big and had a glass in it. It opened into a lobby where the floors were shiny and smelled of floor polish.

We were seated at a dark square table with heavy wooden chairs. I sat across from my father. He ordered drinks and food for all of us. I remember the drink set before me was orange. My father said, "Watch out for Lester--he has never had pop before." I took my first sip which went up my nose and made everyone laugh.

A new taste for a new day and a new world.

Talking - "Dog"

We moved into a big white house on the bend of the James River in the northwest corner of Jamestown. The house faced east onto a gravel road that was Fourth Avenue Northwest.   The morning sun would shine through a big window which looked out over the front porch.

Wayne and I were sitting on the steps of the porch when a dog wandered into our front yard. My brother was trying to teach me to speak. I was two and had never spoken a word. He said, "That's a DOG!" I responded with, "Dog!"

He ran into the house shouting, "He can talk, he can talk!" They came outside to see this wonder.

"Can you talk?"

I repeated, "Dog." Then I said, "Wayne, Ma, Pa, house, cat," and dozens of other words I had saved up for just this event. It has been noted that this was the beginning of a long career of too many words.

The Four Letter Word

Some days later Wayne and I were sitting on those same front steps when several neighbor boys came by to visit. A friendly farmer had brought his bull by to service our milk cow. The old folks were in the kitchen around the big oak table drinking coffee.

The boys began to laugh, point and talk as they watched the barnyard action. They said the "Four Letter Word." This new word must be good. I walked up the stairs and into where the adults were sitting. They were looking out the north window.

I loudly announced that I knew what was going on out in the barnyard. I said, "They are ...." My father said, "Don't say that word in front of your mother."

My mother's face turned a bright red, something that I had never seen before. I went outside and down the steps to tell the boys not to say that word in front of my mother.

Christmas Lights

We set up our Christmas tree in the front room next to our stand-alone radio. I remember being able to count the string of lights. There were seven colored lights covered by white glass bells with pictures of Popeye, Wimpy, Olive Oil, Sweet Pea and others. Silver strands of tinsel hung in rows between brightly colored ornaments.

One snowy Christmas Eve our parents sat us down and explained that Santa was not coming this year. Times were hard but we would still have plenty to eat   Later that evening we heard stomping on our front porch. When my father opened the door, there was a tall man in a uniform covered with snow. In a low voice he asked if this was where the Anderson family lived. He had come by to drop off some things at our neighbor's house, but they were not at home. He asked if we could use some groceries.

He gave my mother a big cardboard box and suggested that the boys go out to the kitchen and check it out. We had a great time. I counted fourteen boxes of Jell-O and piles of canned goods.

More people came in the front door. We heard whispers and someone going up our front steps to the upstairs bedrooms. They left as quickly as they had come. I asked my mother who they were. She said, "They were from God's Army." In the morning presents were under the tree, a tricycle for me and something for everyone else.

The Boulder's Black Dog

The Boulders lived north of our place across from our potato field. Good folks, but their big black lab, Jinks, was the terror of the neighborhood. We would cross to the other side of the road when he was in the yard chained or unchained.

One day Mrs. Boulder told my mother that I should come to her house for a children's *Bible* class. When I got there the dog was gone. Seven or eight boys and girls were there, and we heard *Bible* stories, sang songs and had cookies and punch. She was very nice.

Later in the summer Wayne and I attended *Bible* school at her church which was on Third Avenue by the candy store. We were given a penny for church and a penny for the candy store--at least that is the way I looked at it. Wayne went with the older kids upstairs, while I was sent downstairs with the little kids, where we heard *Bible* stories, sang happy songs, colored pictures and had cookies and punch. The classroom, which smelled of fresh paint, was blue with blue chairs, blue tables, blue benches, and white curtains.

The ladies asked us to kneel at the benches for prayer. One of the ladies said we should close our eyes and fold our hands because we were going to speak to God. She said that Jesus would be here to hear us pray. I closed my eyes and waited. It was very quiet as the lady begun to pray. I peeked through my folded hands. Jesus did not come into the room.

I told my mother that I didn't want to go back to that church even if it was next to the candy store. Mrs. Boulder's boy, Harold, was the leader of a gang of boys, and I did think he needed to go back to Sunday school.

Checker Champ

My brother Wayne had won the city checker championship at the Salvation Army youth center. His prize and recognition were to be given out during Sunday school on Sunday morning. Not being a member he didn't want to go alone. I was five and would go anywhere there might be candy. We walked down town and turned at the old Blackstone Hotel, as the Army was down two blocks by the train station. When we went inside, they put us up front in special chairs.

The whole place was rocking with happy singing, a piano playing, and a drum beating. Wayne went up to the platform and received a box of checkers and a checkerboard. They wrote down our names and invited us to come back to Sunday school.

I liked this place and came back often.   Wayne came back to the youth center but not to Sunday school. A big blue Desoto car came by and picked up me and the Perry kids each week.   The captain was the big man in uniform who came to our door on Christmas Eve. I liked God's Army. I went there until we moved out west, and went again with the Perrys when we returned in 1946. That was my beginning as a believer in what the Salvation Army had to offer.

The Girl I'm Going to Marry

On my walk home at noon from my first week of grade school I didn't know how I was going to tell my mother the good news. As I crossed the old rickety car bridge and stepped onto the dusty gravel road, I thought it would be best just to come right out with it.

I walked around to the back door, went up the steps, opened the door and found my mother standing over the cookstove with a spatula in her hand making pancakes. I have been told that I had called pancakes "a plate full of joy."

I informed her I had wonderful news, "I found the girl I am going to marry." Her name was Rosine Herttel. She lived three blocks away in a green and white house over by the river.

My mother smiled and said, "We'll see. Aren't you a little young for that?"

No, I told her that I thought Rosine said she would marry me. I was six years old. My mother was right again. A week later Rosine had found a new boyfriend, and I had met a new girl to marry.

The first grade was a wonderful place to pick up girls.

Eight Years Old

Bobby, one of my friend Jimmy's brothers, was eight years old. He was rich, tough and knew all the good swear words. I wanted to be eight, but I was only six. At my last birthday party I had gotten a Mounds candy bar, a comb, and a flashlight.

Bobby had money, muscles and macho, before macho was even a word. One day he was in our yard showing us all his money. Something happened and he dropped it on the ground. Everyone got down to help him. A one-dollar bill blew under my shoe--I stood there and waited until every one had gone. I picked up the bill and went downtown to spend it. I met a friend and told him of my stroke of luck. He helped me use up some of my money.

When I got home later that afternoon, Bobby was there talking to my dad. My friend had told him about the dollar. My father said, "Did you take Bobby's money?" I hung my head and said, "Yes."

My father opened his coin purse and took out one dollar, a considerable amount of money in the late 1930s. He gave it to me to give to Bobby with these words: "Lester, Andersons don't do things like that. Tell him you're sorry and you won't do it again."

I was sorry and I did give him the dollar. When I became eight, I checked with Bobby and he told me he had become ten.

Smoking in the Park

South of our house a lane ran along the river through a grove of chokecherry bushes into what we called Studebaker Park. There were tall elm trees, gooseberry bushes, pillars from an old swinging bridge and plenty of green grass. The river made a horseshoe bend to the east under the car bridge, and the gravel road became blacktop across the bridge where Fourth Avenue ran by Washington Grade School to the main part of town. As city water stopped with the blacktop, wells and outhouses were near every house in our neighbor hood.

Harold Boulder, who was thirteen years old at the time, had gone down to the Red Owl grocery store and stolen a carton of Lucky Strike cigarettes. He brought them to the park where Jimmy and I along with another boy were waiting to learn how to smoke. When Harold arrived, he gave each of us two packs. He opened one of his packs and showed us how to light up. Smoke filled the air.

No more picking up cigarette butts off the street or rolling our own with tree leaves and newspaper. This was the real thing. We smoked on and on. Some cigarettes were dropped on the ground half smoked. Things were going as planned. There were plenty of smokes for everyone.

Before noon I headed home covered by the smell of smoke. My mother said I looked sick. I tried to eat but couldn't. As the night wore on, I grew sicker and sicker. My bed was by a window that was partly open. The next morning I could hear Harold yelling, "Come on, Anderson. We're going on a picnic; we've got hotdogs and plenty to eat." What little that was left in my system went out the window onto the front porch roof. It was another day before I could eat anything.

I never ever wanted to smoke again.

Fishing for Profit

In the summer I tried to fish every day. An old cane pole, kite or store string, a nut or bolt for a weight and a ten cent box of hooks made my day. A cork, a can of worms and a spot along the bank where my casting would not get into the trees helped a lot. One day a man in a green car drove into our yard, got out and came over to see my catch. All I had in the washtub was a handful of small shiners. It had been a bad day.

He asked," Kid, do you want to sell your fish?"

"I hope to catch some bigger fish soon. You could come back later."

"No, no, I want these fish. I'll give you a nickel apiece."

I sold him five for twenty-five cents. He put them in a bucket, said he would come back next week, and drove away. He came back every week for awhile and took all the shiners I had. One day he drove in the yard and asked me to come over to his car to see what he had caught with my shiners. On the back floor was the largest fish I had ever seen. He said it was over seven pounds. He had caught it in Spiritwood Lake that morning.

CHAPTER TWO

FOOD

The Old Weathered Barn

The barn was northwest of the house with room for two cows, two horses, chickens, rabbits, pigeons and a load of hay. We boys spent time on those cold days in the winter playing in the hay. A door opened from the cattle stalls into a chicken coop filled with roosting hens. They laid their eggs in wooden boxes fastened to the wall. It took some skill to remove the eggs without getting pecked.

A small opening led from the coop down a short ramp to a fenced in chicken yard. I delighted in crawling in and out through this opening like the chickens.

At night when the cows were milked, my brother and I could stand and watch by the light of the kerosene lanterns. The smells of the cattle, horses, chickens and the lantern are still with me to this day.

Tending the livestock was a full time job which our parents did well. Their stewardship also included two small boys.

My Mother's Pie

My mother could bake pie. Apple, lemon, banana cream, chocolate, mincemeat and pumpkin were on our menu many times. One problem that I did not know about until I ate someone else's pie was--it was the crust that made all the difference. She made what she called healthy crust, plenty of milk. It was tough and substantial. I still miss my mother's pie.

One fall we had a great crowd come to our house for one of those festive occasions. Cousins by the dozens had converged on our house. Every family brought something for the dinner. The pies were put on a table out in our summer kitchen. Two of my cousins and I took three of the pumpkin pies and started for the barn. We decided that we would each eat a pie. We had a table knife so we each started on our pie. One, two, three pieces and I was done. We were all stuffed, our eyes were bigger than our stomachs.

Some one called from the back porch, "Time to come and eat now, boys!" We went in but we didn't eat much. We put the empty pie pans back on the table. I don't think that anyone missed the lost pies.

Potatoes

My grandfather was a potato farmer in Minnesota and must have taught my father how it was done. When we first moved to town, I remember my father walking behind the horses as they plowed the field and later in the summer pulled the potato digger.

We spent time hoeing weeds, especially morning glories beautiful to look at but not good for the potatoes. Cutworms were another big problem. We planted sixteen acres, which ran from Fourth Avenue to Anderson's hill. (Anderson's hill, still called that to this day, is the place we all went sliding in the winter.)

My father would sell potatoes for about a dollar a hundred pounds. What we didn't sell we saved for seed or for the family. They were put down the coal chute into our dirt cellar. Potatoes were never washed for storage. Carrots, onions, parsnips and beets were also stored in or under gunny sacks. When the vegetables were safely put away, a load of lignite coal would be sent down the coal chute to fill up the cellar.

Johnny Cake

Johnny cake, a type of corn bread, was made in a large pan and served with butter and syrup. Corn meal mush, oatmeal, cream of wheat and sometimes cornflakes were on the breakfast table. Pancakes were eaten Swedish style with milk and sugar any time of the day. Eggs and salt pork with toast, made by putting the bread on top of the cookstove, could be eaten early or late.

Grape and strawberry jelly, white and dark syrup in half gallon cans, crocks of sour cream and homemade butter could be found in the cupboard in the back kitchen next to the cookstove. I remember chicken and homemade dumplings, loaves of hot bread every week, and fried strips of bread dough covered with white sugar.

A big black frying pan with five pounds of lard was bubbling away as piles of nutmeg donuts were laid out on a wax paper covered table every month. Those that weren't eaten hot were put in a big crock with a lid to be used as dunkers.

Bowls of rice covered with milk, sugar, butter and cinnamon were common on our table. The coffee pot was always on. Plenty to eat even through the bleak days of the depression.

The Garden of Life

East of the gray barn was a large black dirt garden plot that we planted every year.   Peas, carrots, onions, potatoes, ground cherries, cucumbers, lettuce, tomatoes, dill weed, parsnips, cabbage, green beans, navy beans, corn, beets and sometimes melons were planted row upon row.

During the winter months buckets of wastewater were poured on the snow where the garden was to be. Fertilizer from the barn was put on at the first sign of spring.

A friend of my father would come by with his little Ford garden tractor and prepare the ground for planting. My mother would save seeds by drying them on newspapers and putting them away in labeled jars. With that work and conditioning it's no wonder that our vegetables were great every year.

I remember at an early age that with great haste all the vegetables were canned for the cold winter months. The garden was tended as if our lives depended on it. We enjoyed a good table because the old folks knew enough to get ready for the winter.

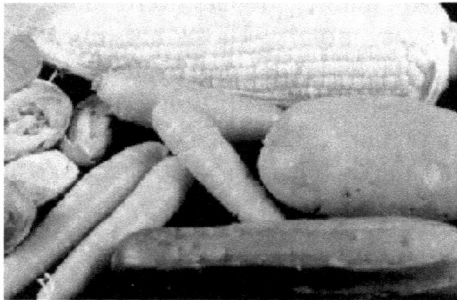

Fish in a Barrel

Like most Swedish immigrants my father was fond of pickled herring. When the weather turned cold, he would come home with a large jar of herring to be enjoyed by all the family. Some winters we would get a barrel of frozen herring which was kept outdoors along the north side of the house in one of the big snowdrifts. A board that was used as a cover was held down by a large rock to keep the varmints away.

Our house was a popular stopping-off place for the many relatives and old farm friends who came to Jamestown for shopping and taking care of business. For some reason they came mostly when we were getting ready to eat.

One of my jobs was to count the people who would be eating with us and bring in enough fish for supper. I needed an ice pick to chip the frozen fish from the block of ice they were in.

My mother would take her large black frying pan and fill it with fish to fry. The rest of the meal consisted of fried potatoes, peas, bread and coffee. Some were served fried roe (fish eggs) which showed up when the fish were cleaned. The barrel must have held several hundred fish because it lasted most of the winter.

Pumping Crabs

Little boys need to do things little girls don't do. Pumping crabs was a thing this little boy liked to do that no little girl in our part of town would ever do. The crawfish that we called crabs were plentiful along the banks of the James River in mounds easy to spot. It took only a stick and a can for water to conquer this demon of the deep.

The pile of mud over their hole would be pushed aside, and another hole was made with a stick a few inches higher away from the water. Then water was poured into either hole and the stick was pumped up and down. In a short while the crawfish would emerge from the hole. The pumper would pick it up and move on to the next hole. When enough had been collected for those eaters present, a fire was started and the tails were boiled in salty water and eaten.

Sometimes we cooked field corn at the same time. We would place a gallon can filled with corn and water over the fire. When the water boiled over, the corn was done. We baked potatoes by putting them in the dirt under the fire or by dropping them in the dying embers. Every so often they came out as black as charcoal. In the evening we would build bonfires and make torches by dipping cattails, found at the water's edge, in kerosene. Everyone with a torch would help light up the sky.

CHAPTER THREE

NOTABLE PEOPLE

Two Blondes

In the summer of 1937 I would cruise the neighborhood with my tricycle trying to pick up girls. I remember not being old enough to go to school. When all the kids went by on their way to school, I would get out my wheels and go around the block. Several blocks away to the northeast in a small two-room tarpaper shack lived two blond curly haired sisters. They were also not old enough for grade school.

I would go by and give them a ride up and down their street. One would ride on the handlebars, and the other would stand on the back with her hands on my shoulders. One day I took them by the house to see my mother. She gave us some cookies and said what nice girls they were. When I came home, she told me that their father was in prison, but I was not to tell them that I knew about it.

The next time I picked them up, the first thing I said was, "Is your father in prison?" They both cried and went home. Years later I graduated with the younger sister. She turned out to be a lovely lady.

Hallelujah, I'm a Bum

Upstairs in the southwest corner of our big white house was an unfinished storage area where we could play during bad weather days. Time was spent playing one of two records we had on an old windup phonograph. One side had a song that started with the sound of men marching. When they stopped, they began singing

"Tenting tonight in the old campground." On the other side of the record a man sang, "I went to a house, and I asked for some bread, and the lady said, 'Bum bum, the baker is dead.' Hallelujah, I'm a bum, hallelujah bum again, hallelujah, give a hand out to revive us again."

Many summer days I recall my mother asking me to go out to the barn to get eggs so she could feed some hungry man who had come to our back kitchen door. She never turned them away, and could always fix something substantial to add with those eggs like fried potatoes, buttered toast and coffee. Our house must have been marked with a special sign because we lived a mile from the railroad tracks.

Some of her goodness may have rubbed off on me. I spent years helping what was then called "bums" make their way down the tracks to a better life. Hallelujah, we gave a hand out to revive them again.

Old Lady Pickard

We would call out to her as she scurried by our house, "Old Lady Pickard, Old Lady Pickard!" Then the neighbor boys and I would throw rocks or gravel at her. She would not stop and would pretend that she didn't hear what we were yelling. She looked something like the Wicked Witch of the North in the *Wizard of Oz*. She was dressed in black from head to toe.

We could almost set our clock by the time she came by each day. Coming home in the afternoon, she would be carrying a paper bag in one hand and a bundle of sticks under her other arm.

One morning our family was shopping downtown at the Red Owl grocery store when Miss Pickard came in. The store had a small counter just inside the front door where they served lunch. Their special in the morning was two donuts and a cup of coffee for five cents. We watched as Miss Pickard waited for a customer to get up and leave their empty cup and part of a donut.

As the patron exited the store, she quickly moved on to their stool and pushed the cup forward, took a bite of the donut, saying,

"I'll have some more coffee." The clerk said, "Why don't I give you a fresh cup and a couple more donuts?" Someone remarked that she did this almost every day.

Some years later while visiting the new owners of the Fourth Avenue Roadhouse, I saw Old Lady Pickard hanging some things on a clothesline and asked who she was. "Oh," he said, "That's Miss Pickard, a retired schoolteacher. She is over ninety and has been stone deaf for years. She lives alone in a small apartment out back."

Colored Water

I discovered the bright world of color when I was five years old. If you soaked colored crepe paper in water long enough, it would give off a long lasting bright color. If you mixed red and yellow, the water would turn orange. Yellow and blue would turn the water green. Red and blue would make purple.

In the summer I spent time mixing colors on our front porch. The only clear bottles were those I found along the side of the road: wine, whiskey, gin and a variety of other bottles that had contained alcoholic beverages. I begin to line up the bottles on the porch rail so that the sun would dance the colors on the floor. I had fifteen or more. What a glorious display. I was the king of color.

A car drove up in the driveway. A man in a black suit, a white shirt and tie got out and went to our front door. He rapped on the door, and my mother let him in. In a little while he came out, got in his car and left.

My mother came out onto the front porch and waved good-by as he drove away. She stared at my colored bottles with a surprised look on her face. "Lester, what have you done? That was the Lutheran minister; he must think we are all drunks." She helped me empty the bottles and fix up the porch.

Dutch Henry

Dutch Henry lived in a red railroad cookcar that had been made into a house. His yard was sheltered by a row of trees to the east along Third Avenue Northwest. On the south his large garden went down to the road that ran along the James River. On the west was a chain link fence that went half the length of his yard.

His nephew, who worked for the fire department, would bring a fire-engine down to the river several times a month and flush his hoses over Dutch's garden. Our mother also said he fertilized it with something she called night soil. His crop of vegetables was outstanding and the envy of the entire neighborhood. His beets would be the size of other people's melons.

He was almost five feet tall and weighed over three hundred pounds. Most of the time during the summer months he wore a pair of work shoes, old blue bib overalls, a slouch hat and little more. My friend Jimmy and I would come over to his house just to watch him eat. It was said that he could eat a whole cooked chicken by himself at one time.

After eating he would take a nap in his hammock strung between two trees in his front yard. When he would get in, the trees would bend and the gray canvas hammock would almost touch the ground. We also liked to sit and listen to him snore. At times he would take a chew of snuff from a little round box. Shortly the snuff would be running down the side of his face onto his chin. He had a spit can on the ground at one end of the hammock.

One day while he was sleeping, his snuffbox dropped to the ground. When he went to his outhouse to relieve himself, we decided it was time to try some of his snuff. We both took a big chew. In a few minutes we were gagging and had turned green. We spit all the way to the pump where we washed out our mouths and pledged that we would leave the snuff to Dutch.

That was the first and last time I ever tried snuff. I was seven years old.

Louie Coop

Louie Coop came by our house to visit two or three times a month. He lived downtown and was always welcomed by my parents. His pale face was clean-shaven. He was bald with a little white hair on each side of his head. He was soft spoken with some kind of speech impediment; he stuttered and shuffled his feet when he walked. He was at all times clean and well dressed.

Louie was an artist. When he came I would ask him to make a picture for me. With a piece of cardboard and a small jackknife he would cut into the cardboard a picture of ocean waves, sailboats, clouds and sea gulls. Sometimes he would make trees, hills and houses.

He always came in time for dinner. He left as quickly as he came. Years later when I was helping at the Salvation Army the Captain was reading a list of soldiers.

"Does anyone know who Louie Coop was?"

I raised my hand and said I knew him personally.   Someone else said he had died in a rest home.

Jimmy and the Red Owl Store

Jimmy came by our house one Saturday morning on his way to work as a box boy at the Red Owl grocery store. I was eight years old. I asked what he got paid and could they use another boy. He said he didn't know what the pay was, but he was sure they could use another box boy. I told my mother I was going with Jimmy and would be back soon. When we got to the store, an older boy told us what to do. We put out boxes and canned goods on the empty shelves.

When we were called, we would help carry boxes full of groceries. What fun, and we were getting paid for it. At closing time the doors were locked.

We went to the office to get paid. Mr. Potter was at his desk. He turned and said, "What do you boys want?"

Jimmy said we had worked all day.

He said, "Who hired you? Well OK, here's a quarter."

We took our one quarter and headed for the door. Jimmy said not to mind, we did good work. When we got out the back door to the alley, he told me to follow him. He led me over to a fence where old signs were stacked up. Behind the signs I saw a box full of cookies, candy and other good things to eat. He pulled back a tarp covering several more boxes. He had been packing boxes for himself. When he carried out a box, he took one for himself. He took some items and covered the other boxes for later.

Potter saved a lot of money by paying Jimmy a quarter. On the way home we crossed the tracks by the grain elevator and discovered that it was on fire. The fire trucks came and the crowd gathered. We stayed until the fire was out. We got home after nine. My folks were ready to call the police and drag the river.

I never told them about the boxes.

CHAPTER FOUR

NOTABLE ANIMALS

My cousin Skipper Zurn and I are standing on the boxes. Cousin DeWayne Anderson, John and Emma's son who stayed with us one year is the boy sitting on the fence.

Beans

Beans was a dog that would eat anything but beans. He could run and jump as high as the kitchen table. I don't remember when or where he came from. He looked like a Boston terrier. It seemed to me that we had always had him.

One of my cousins raised terriers, and he might have given him to us. I have been told that one rainy day they saw smoke coming from his doghouse. When they looked inside, he and I were sitting around a fire roasting hot dogs. They got us out just in time. I don't know how that dog learned to start a fire.

Another time I had taken a ring of bologna, tied it to a string, and he chased me and the bologna around the room until my mother saw what was happening and stopped us.

When Wayne, Beans and I would make too much noise, we would be given "time out" by our older brother, Leonard. He would make us each sit on a chair in our own corner. Beans would sit on his chair with tears in his eyes and only get down when he was told to.

By the time we got ready to move to the west coast when I was ten, we had another dog.

What is an Outhouse?

An outhouse is a toilet without plumbing or running water. It was out away from the house because of the smell, but close enough to make it easy to get to during cold and rainy days. There were one holers, two holers, and three holers. Sometimes there was a lid to cover the holes. Most of the time the holes were hand carved in a pine board. The Sears' and Montgomery Ward's catalogs were used as toilet paper and reading material at the same time. During fruit season we moved up a notch and had the wrappings that the peaches came in. Some rich folks had rolls of toilet paper reserved for guests. The deluxe models had shelves where lime was stored to be sprinkled in the holes each day.

We had a two-holer-regular-people model. It was down by the river not too far from our well. You could see out through the cracks in the door which was locked with an eye and hook. When someone was inside and you approached, they might cough or start singing. You had to wait your turn. The reason for the two holes was to make the best use of the space below. At least once a year a new outhouse hole was dug. It could be to either side or in front, never in back. The dirt from the new hole was used to fill the old hole.   Rhubarb or horseradish might be planted in the fertile ground.

One day when I was seven years old, I was playing with one of our "kids." Our nanny goat had given birth to two male goats that had grown in one year to be almost as big as their mother. I was twisting the biggest one's head as I gripped his horns. It seems he had had enough of my rough play and thought it was time to get even with me. When I let go, he backed up and charged knocking me to the ground. I got up and tried to grab his horns. He ducked his head and hit me again. I began to call him names and call for help. No help came.

He chased me around the yard. The only place to escape to was the open outhouse. I ran inside and tried to lock the door. He hit it with a bang. The door flew open and he charged inside. I jumped up on the pine board hoping to miss the holes. He hit the side again and again. He backed up to get a good run to get up to where I was hanging on. When he got outside, I hopped down and locked the door. He hit the door several times and then went back to his mother. I waited and then ran into the house to my mother.

Following that adventure I kept a stick by the door that I used to whack him when I went outside. After a while we left each other alone.

Why Did The Chicken...?

Why does a chicken do anything? As early as I can remember, we had a flock of chickens. Rhode Island Reds and the black and white Plymouth Rocks laid brown eggs and topped out at about three to four pounds. The white Leghorns laid white eggs and weighed about two pounds. Each spring our mother would order one hundred little Leghorn chicks that would mature by fall and be canned for winter consumption. During the summer months they were our fryers.

 One of our Rhode Island Red hens had gone off into the brush to lay her eggs and hatch her young. My mother said that we were not to worry; she would return home in a week or two when the young had hatched.

Several weeks later my good friend Jimmy and I were walking along the river looking for a new spot to fish. We passed by old George Seekerson's place, a little white house, a small shed and a fenced-in area where he kept a few chickens. He had from time to time put out a live animal trap used to catch raccoons. There in the fenced-in area was our big red hen and her brood of chicks. George had never had a chicken that looked like our hen.

I hurried home and told my mother, who in turn told my father. He took a cardboard box and started up the road toward Seekerson's house. George came to the door. My father questioned him about the chickens which he said were his. My dad was twice the size of George--when he suggested that he had a way to solve the problem, George was willing to listen. The hen and her chicks would be placed in the box and taken to the bend in the road half way between his place and ours. Whomever the chickens followed home would be the owner.

George hemmed and hawed for a minute and then agreed. When we arrived at the spot, the chickens were put out on the road. George and my father talked for a little while and then parted. The chickens scratched in the dust for a few moments. As we walked toward our house, the hen and all her little chicks turned and followed us home. I thought my dad was so smart.

Our Cow is Gone

It was a cold rainy day. Our Swiss cow had been put out to pasture on a grassy hillside. My father was standing on the front porch in the early evening looking for her as the lightning was flashing. He said he saw her on top of the hill. As the lightning flashed, we could see a small coupe car and two men pushing a cow into a trailer. In a moment they were gone. The next morning our cow did not come home. My parents supposed that someone had taken her. We had one cow left, but she was not producing enough milk for our family. My father informed the sheriff's office; even though they were able to find tire tracks, they had no way to help us.

At that time my father was working as a grader for Porter Brothers' Hide and Fur Company out by the roundhouse. One day while he was grading cattle hides, he recognized the hide of our Swiss cow. As she was our main milk cow, he had spent considerable time looking at the pattern on her side at milking time. He checked with the office and found the name of the person who had sold this hide. He called the sheriff and pressed charges against the man.

Days had passed when the sheriff's car pulled up in our yard. Two men got out of the car and came over to where my father and I were standing. I remember that my mother had made me a pair of bib overalls that looked just like my dad's. As the sheriff talked and the man in the blue suit stood looking at the ground, my father put his thumbs under his suspenders and pushed out. I did the same. We were going to make a deal.

The sheriff asked that all charges be dropped against this man because he was sorry. His family would suffer if he had to go to prison. He was willing to pay twice the price of a new cow. My father agreed to settle for about $140. This pleased the sheriff and the man looked up and smiled. He took the money out of an envelope and gave the cash to my dad. They got back into the car and drove away. I said to my father, "I could have a dollar?" He said, "We'll see."

Years later while visiting family in Jamestown, I heard that this cattle thief and his brother had been elected to public office. I won't say what their party affiliation was, but I wouldn't have voted for them.

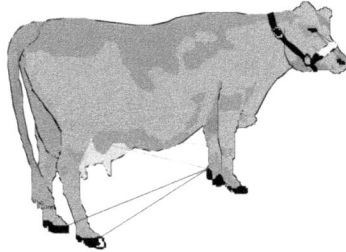

The Cow in the River

My dad, Wayne and some family friends had gone skunk hunting. The ladies and a flock of kids were all over to our house while they waited for them to return. The call came out that one of our milk cows had fallen into the river. She had slipped while getting a drink and had broken her neck.

Milk cows were often more like family, and my mother dreaded having to kill it. She went around the neighborhood trying to find a man to do it. None had the nerve or skill to do it.

My mother asked someone to go to the kitchen to get a butcher knife. There in front of a crowd of people she stood in the river mud and bled the cow to save the meat from spoiling. I stood on the bank with the ladies and other children and in a loud voice declared, "Don't be afraid, ladies. I'll protect you."

The skunk hunters returned with a tub full of freshly killed stinkers. When my mother told my father about the cow, he said she had done the right thing. There were more comments about my statement around the supper table that evening than there were about the cow or the skunks.

Jimmy, the Crow

The Fetz family, living on the corner of highway 281 and Fourth Avenue Northwest, had a cage out by their garage where they kept their pet crow, "Jimmy." It was said that he had a split tongue that made it possible for him to talk.

Many days he would fly over to Washington Grade School when the students were at recess on the playground. He hopped from group to group looking for something to steal. Jimmy fluttered away when someone tried to pick him up or threw something at him. He was a larger than usual shiny black crow who could say "Hello" or let out a string of phrases that sounded like swear words to the teachers. He looked for marbles and shiny objects from the gangs of children at play. When they were pitching pennies, he would take the one that got away. He would fly off with his prize, only to return for more when he had stashed it away.

One day I gave him half a Tootsie Roll. He followed me home and came and sat on my arm. The next morning and for weeks later, he was sitting on the clothesline post ready to go to school with me. I saved candy for him.

One warm spring morning when the third grade teacher had raised the window to let in the warm air, he came to the windowsill. He hopped back and forth saying, "Hello, hello, hello." The teacher went to the window to chase him away when he let out his string of swear words. We laughed and the teacher closed the window. I was told years later that he had lived to be thirty-nine years old.

By the way Bobby married Edna, the Fetz's daughter.

CHAPTER FIVE

AN ADVENTURE FILLED LIFE

King Kong

My sisters, Blanche and Gladys, took me to see my first movie. We walked downtown to the Jamestown Theater, which had a large monster ape with glowing red eyes out front. It was daytime so I could see that he was not real. We went inside and sat with a crowd of people. I thought the events that took place were real.

When I got home, I told my mother in great detail all the actions that had taken place in the movie. My sisters said that I remembered most of the facts. It was a good thing that I had learned to talk by that time.

I saw that giant ape from time to time in my dreams. My sisters married in 1936. The movie *King Kong* came out in 1933 and must have arrived in Jamestown some time in 1934. My best guess is that I saw it in the summer of 1935 when I was three years old. I remember coming home to the house in Jamestown.

My sisters were always happy around me. They smelled good and dressed in pretty clothes. Blanche was diabetic and died in childbirth in 1938, and the baby died soon after. Blanche had been married for two years to Al Shocker, who was Jewish and worked at the railroad coal yards with members of his family.

At the funeral my father held me up so I could see her in the coffin. Everybody around me was crying. My father said to my mother that I didn't know what was going on.

I didn't, but I cried anyway.

Black Blizzards

During the dirty thirties' winters there were high winds with very little snow. The temperature would drop way below zero with winds of thirty to forty miles an hour. When the black blizzards came, it was necessary to turn on all the lights in the house during the day. The black snow would come in through the window and door sills. In the afternoon it would be as dark as night outside. You could not see your hand in front of your face. When the winds stopped, there would be black snow banks.

The white snow might come with the next blizzard and cover the black banks. On the days when we went outside to play, we would make forts by cutting blocks out of the snow banks. The blocks looked like layer cakes with streaks of white and black. Many farms lost a great deal of topsoil during those years.

Singing from Across the River

On warm summer evenings we would listen to the beautiful songs of Zion floating through the elm trees across the river into our backyard. It was revival meeting time at the Holiness Camp Grounds. The singing always impressed me and made a lasting impact which remains with me to this day. As early as I can remember, my mother and father would go over to the camp meetings to see old friends from the country. The camp was in a horseshoe bend of the river surrounded by water with campsites for over two hundred people.

We would walk down to the car bridge, cross over and take the first road to the right. I remember that most of the time we would stay for the singing in the big meeting hall. The floor was covered with sawdust, and we all sat on wooden benches. The sides of the hall could be raised to let in the cool night air.

Special groups and soloists sang church songs. After an hour or so the preacher would get up and preach from his *Bible*. At the end of the meeting they would sing another song, and people would stand and go down to the front to pray.

One of the families that my folks would go by to see was the Johnsons. The Johnsons were an older couple who had no children at home and lived across the river to the west of the campground. They would always give us a little lunch. We would get to their house by going over a swinging bridge. They called it swinging because it was made of boards tied together and held up by ropes that swayed back and forth when you walked on it. We had to hold on to the ropes and sometimes crossed over one at a time. We went to those meeting most summers until 1942 when we moved out west.

Stars in the Sky

Directly across from our house to the east was a small white stucco house with green trim. The Slushers, Fenners, Cumbers, and Perrys lived there during the years we resided on Fourth Avenue. Back of the house was an outhouse and a small garage that served as a utility shed most of the time. We boys would lay on the roof, hidden away from the world, in the early evening and watch for falling stars.

When the Aurora Borealis, the Northern Lights, would be putting on a display, we would spend hours lying there talking about what there was and what there might be. The dancing lights would be red, blue, white and green and some nights form a dome that surrounded us on all sides.

The sky in those days was very clear, one of those places you could see forever. It was almost as if you would fall off the end of the earth. We could find the Big and Little Dipper, the North Star, and some constellations. We talked of Buck Rogers and his flights to outer space, which we knew could never be. Everything seemed so small when we were looking at the stars and the wonders of the heavens.

Two Egg Movies

In the thirties Jamestown had three theaters. North on Main Street there was the Grand Theater, which had a balcony and charged as much as fifty cents for the better movies. South across the tracks by the post office was the Jamestown Theater, which showed both "A" and "B" movies and cost as much a twenty-five cents. Around the corner behind Pred's Women's Clothing Store and across the street from the S. & L. Department Store, was the Star Theater, which showed mostly "B" movies.

Kids under twelve paid ten cents even for a double feature. During hard times their special kid's price was two eggs and a nickel. My friend came by our house on the way to the picture show with two nickels. I went to the barn where I picked up the four eggs. We rode off on our imaginary horses to the Saturday western. Those were the days.

The Lone Ranger

Radio was our window to the world of imagination. "Good Morning, Breakfast Clubbers, we're here to greet you" was sung every weekday morning by Don McNeal from Chicago. Then *Fiction and Fact from Sam's Almanac* came on followed by the morning news.

In the early afternoon my mother listened to *Old Ma Perkins, the Guiding Light, Helen Trent* and a host of others. After the soap operas came the kids' programs, *Jack Armstrong, Superman, Tom Mix* and many more.

Early in the evening when the lights were low, the Lone Ranger would come thundering into our front room from out of the past. It was a good reason for me to come into the house at dusk. I was the Lone Ranger. When I was five or six, I cut a mask from the lining of my mother's best coat which I had found hanging in our upstairs storage room.

One day someone told me where the radio station was that broadcast these stories. A friend and I walked downtown across the railroad tracks and found the station at the bottom of the hill by the river. We climbed the stairs to the second floor where we knocked on the door and asked to see the Lone Ranger.

The man said, "Come in, boys. I'll get him for you." He returned with a big envelope. He opened it and took out a very large phonograph record. He grinned, "Boys, this is the Lone Ranger." He told us that these records came in the mail each week.

He was alone and asked us to listen to him give the news. After the news he played some music. While it was playing, he showed us the rest of the station. As we were going out the door, he said we could come back again, which we did often.

Three City Parks

McElroy, Klaus, and Nicholas were all good places for family reunions. Most of the time thirty or forty relatives would meet at McElroy Park in July for an annual picnic. The Fourth of July was always a special day because the fair grounds were covered with exhibits and the rides came to town. Frequently the rain came too.

As Nicholas Park was near our house, we spent many days playing there. Swings, slides, wading pools and organized games by the city parks department were all waiting for us. At night a footbridge that opened onto Main Street four blocks from downtown became a lover's park.

The older boys played strip poker on the tables at the north end of the park. My friend Jimmy lost all his clothes and was made to run nude around the pine trees down to the outhouses and back to get his clothes back.

John Ferguson, one of the rowdy boys, jumped off the table with a pocket knife in his hand and stabbed my brother Wayne above the eye. He bled and I cried. He survived with no damage to that eye.

One day we went swimming at Klaus Park, blocks away south across the tracks. When we arrived at the bath house, the door was blocked. A boy was changing and wouldn't let anyone in. We waited and pounded on the door. After fifteen minutes he came dashing out totally nude and jumped in the pool. He had forgotten his suit and didn't think it was right to undress in public. We all laughed, and the ladies made him go back and put on his clothes.

The BB Gun Wars

"Boys, don't shoot the birds!" not, "You'll shoot your eye out," is what our mother would say as my brother Wayne and I took our BB guns out the door. We had both shot .22 rifles by the time we were five years old. I remember sitting on my father's lap down by the river shooting empty Carnation evaporated milk cans as they floated by in the water. He always said we should consider that every gun was loaded and to never point a loaded or unloaded gun at anyone.

This was the day of the much looked forward to BB gun war that had been talked about and planned for weeks. A group of nine to ten boys met out in the woods at the base of the hill a half mile north of our house. My brother had his Red Rider Daisy 100- shot special. I had the old "Silver Eagle," a no-name one-shot had-seen-better-days BB gun. Sides were chosen by where we lived. I was the youngest and went with my brother's team.

The rules were simple: shoot low, no shots above the belt. One hit and you were dead and out of the game. The team with the last man standing was to be the winner. The other team left. Our group planned their strategy. Some would go up the hill and come in from the back. The others would go along the trees and come in from the south side.

The signal was given for the war to start. What was I to do? I was six and my gun held only one shot. The leader said, "Little Anderson, you hide under that gooseberry bush; shoot whoever comes by in the foot."

They all laughed and left for the war. I got down on the ground and crawled under the bush. It grew very quiet. I could hear the birds that I wasn't supposed to shoot. I cocked my gun. I pointed it toward the path.

The one BB rolled out the barrel and fell into the dust. I scraped around until I found it and put it back into the gun. I had more in my pocket. There was shouting. "You hit me on the head" and "Shoot, shoot, he's over there."

Bang, bang. "We got the last one."

It wasn't anyone from our team that was shouting. They were all dead. "Hey, where is the little Anderson?"

They came down the path and stood by the gooseberry bush. I saw three or four sets of shoes. I pulled the trigger--my gun popped. The one shot rolled out the end of the gun and into the dust. I was done. I came out with my hands above my head.

"We found him; the war is over." My brother came and said we should go home; we had lost. I said, "No one shot me."

He said, "Ah, you don't count." We never told our mother of our war games.

Rubber Guns

During the summer months we boys made rubber guns, slingshots, wooden swords and kites. To make a rubber gun it took a piece of wood about a foot long. We would cut out a handle and a barrel. Strips of rubber would be cut from an old spare inner tube to be used as a binder to hold a snap clothespin to the handle. Other strips were cut for ammunition.

There were many variations; some boys even had a machinegun arrangement. Battles with rubber guns were safer and more fun than BB gun wars.

Slingshots were a different story. The handle would be cut from the crotch of a tree. Some makers would look all day for the perfect handle; then they would climb the tree and cut down the limb. The rubber would be cut from the spare tire tube and the rock holder from an old leather belt or shoe. The slingshot was a dangerous weapon. In the hands of a good marksman it could kill a bird. You could never have a war with a slingshot without someone getting hurt.

The wooden swords were made from laths. A cross handle would be nailed away from the pointed end. To play pirates we would make a shield from a garbage can lid and hack away at each other to our heart's content.

In the fall we made kites from pine sticks and newspaper. The sticks were formed into a cross with the shorter crossbar high on the main stick. A pattern was made and it was all glued together with flour paste, the tail being made of strips of cloth. We tied together what we called store string. Why it flew I know not why, but it did.

The Fourth Avenue Roadhouse

The roadhouse was a large white two-story structure at the end of Fourth Avenue. Beyond here the gravel road climbed up over the hills north of Jamestown onto bleak farmland. It was the oldest building on our end of town and by its appearance had been built at the turn of the century. A porch ran the length of the house on the south side.

To the east were the banks of the long slough where beaver and muskrats built their homes. Up a small hill beyond the slough was a big red barn where horses and cows were stabled. Jimmy's family had moved into the roadhouse.

When I came over to play with him, he took me in and out of the bedroom closets. When the back wall of the closet was pushed, it would open into another bedroom. By placing your ear to the air vents you could hear what people were saying in the other rooms. Four or five bedrooms were on the second floor. The wall at the top of the stairs would swing open to give a hiding place for up to eight people. In a large dining room over twenty people could eat at one time.

In the backyard in a smokehouse and a series of small buildings we spent many hours playing cards and other games with our friends during the cold winter months. We were told that at one time the stagecoach had stopped at the roadhouse.

The James River

We boys were river rats. Our summers were spent riding up and down the river on rafts and later in a white sailboat. My brother Wayne acquired the boat from a friend for one dollar and a stack of worthless comic books. The boat had no sail. We kept running it into the rocks and limbs on the side of the river. As a result we all learned to melt tar in a can over a fire and patch the holes.

We went east through the woods along the river to the old swimming hole where we boys all went skinny-dipping. In the river behind our house I would fish for bullheads, carp, suckers and shiners. We would eat crab tails by boiling them in a can of water over a campfire.

Wayne and I both started skating at an early age. In the winter the kids from the neighborhood would use our summer kitchen cookstove as a place to warm their feet while they drank hot cocoa and ate popcorn. Often there was a gang of kids playing hockey with a tin can and makeshift hockey sticks out behind our house. The frozen river was our road to explore forbidden and friendly places.

We also trapped and hunted along its banks. We could skate for miles in both directions. At times we would be gone for hours. In the spring when the ice was breaking up, we would find great delight by jumping from one ice floe to another.

In the spring and fall great flocks of birds used the river as a flyway. One day I was sitting on a pile of rocks on the river bank, wearing my brother's aviator cap. A large crane hit the top of my head with a deposit as he rose from the water on his way north. I took off and flew into the house.

As senior citizens Wayne and I spent some days finding the source of our river. Every boy should have his own river.

CHAPTER SIX

SEATTLE: THE WAR YEARS

Moving West 1942 to 1946

In the spring of 1942 we packed up our belongings and prepared to move west to help win the war. Dewayne, John and Emma's son who had been living with us, had returned home to Washington. His parents had left him with us for the year because his father had a job that required him to be constantly moving from place to place.

I called DeWayne who was a year older than me, "the pig rider." A pig had wandered into our yard after an accident up on highway 281. We kept it in the yard by the barn. DeWayne had shown us his skill as a bronco buster by riding the pig at will around the yard. He and I had shared mumps, chicken pox and whooping cough that winter. I had attended only forty-six days of school which resulted in my having to repeat the fourth grade when we got to Seattle.

The pig was turned into chops and such after my father had put a notice in the paper looking for the owner. Our neighbor, August Fennern, and my father slaughtered the pig down at their place and split the meat between our families.

Mr. Merchant, who owned our house and the sixteen acres of land that my father truck farmed, offered to sell it all to my father for about four thousand dollars. My father declined the offer saying we had to go help win the war.

As we drove away south across the car bridge over the James River, I remember looking out the back window and seeing my little terrier dog, that I had given to the neighbors, running at full speed in the cloud of dust kicked up by the car. That was my last image of the big white house on Fourth Avenue Northwest.

Leonard, our oldest brother, had joined the army and was somewhere in England waiting as the Allies built up their strength for the invasion of Europe. Before he left I remember my mother giving him a black zipper *Bible* which she said he would need to read.

Wayne had gone out to Seattle on his own a half year earlier to live with our sister Gladys and her husband, Ove Larson, who was working in a war plant in the area. At the time Wayne left he was almost fourteen years old. He had arrived at the train station in Seattle to find no one there to meet him. Not knowing what else to do, he took the bus to the end of the line and began walking. He started down the road dragging his large suitcase behind him. With eight miles to go, a Lutheran minister stopped to pick him up and helped him find our sister's house.

The Train Through the Mountains

The Northern Pacific railroad station at Jamestown was packed. It looked like half the city was moving west to help with the war effort. When we got on the train, we put our boxes, tied with rope, where we could see them. The only piece of furniture we took with us was my mother's Singer sewing machine.

I remember the rocking of the train, miles of wheat fields, the long tunnels, the towering mountain passes, the tall pine forests and having no place to sleep. The smell of the smoke and cinders from the steam engine drifted in through the windows and doors as people moved from car to car. The porters were the first black people that I had ever seen up close.

Everyone was talking about the war. Everyone seemed to be going west to help our soldiers win against the Germans and the Japs. It seemed like days since we had left Jamestown. The fruit and sandwiches we had brought with us were almost gone. We pulled into foggy Seattle to a new world. Soldiers and sailors were everywhere. The cool crisp air smelled of the sea and fish.

Gladys and Ove were there to meet us and take us to their home in Renwood Park. In the distance to the south we had our first look at Mt. Rainer glowing in the morning sun.   As we drove up toward their house, we saw people building everywhere.   The roads were lined with enormous pine trees being felled to make room for all the new people.   The air was cool and filled with the smell of Christmas pine.

Brenmar

Brenmar grade school was held in an old red brick building that had been a school for girls.   It was down the hill from where we were staying with my sister and had room for only the fourth, fifth and sixth grades.   On a large fenced-in playground on the side of the hill with steep banks we played soccer and baseball every day when it didn't rain. Everyone I met was from some place other than Seattle.   The teachers were all glad to see us and tried to help us as much as they could. We talked about the war every day. To get home my friends and I had to walk uphill for eight or nine blocks.

Some days we took a short cut through a farmer's orchard with large delicious apples, pears, apricots and plums in row upon row. I had never seen fruit growing in such abundance. When we asked the farmer if we could have some apples, he said we could as long as we took only the big ones because they were the hardest to sell.

We came that way often. At one point we had to cross a busy highway; when we reached the top of the hill, we would toss our apple cores down on the passing cars.

When winter came it was very different from what we had left behind in North Dakota. The countryside stayed green and didn't get very cold; it just rained every day. The only snow I remember was on Christmas morning. The ground, roofs and fallen trees had a light covering of white until the afternoon.

Art Lessons

My mother was a believer in reading hands. Because my fingers were long, she said I should learn to play the piano or take art lessons. I chose art lessons because we didn't have a piano and I wanted to play baseball as much as I could. The lessons were given by a little old lady in the area. I attended nine classes which cost five dollars each. That, by the way, was a magnificent sum in the days when fifty cents an hour was the going wage.

She showed each of us ten children in the class how to make things look real. By the time I finished the class, I could draw trees, people, fish, boats, the sky and many other things. I knew how to mix colors, make things look near or far away. She made it fun to draw.

We moved the next summer to Renton Highlands, just above the Boeing airplane factory where my folks had gotten jobs helping to make the B-17 bomber. When my fifth grade teacher saw my drawings, she asked me to do the scenery for the school play. For the next two years a boy named Bob Weymouth and I did all the scenery for all of the plays. I still rely on the training I received from that art teacher those many years ago.

The Jones Boys

The Jones boys lived down the road to the east of my sister's house. When the blacktop turned uphill to the right, a dirt road ran back into high woods. They lived in an old log shack with a big open porch with several couches and overstuffed chairs where the family congregated in the evenings. Upon my first visit to their house their mother gave me a large candy bar and said what a nice white boy I was.

The two brothers and I built go-carts which we rode up and down the hills. We spent some Saturdays going down the side of our mountain to visit a farm with several large cherry trees. Some days we stayed in the cherry trees for hours or until the farmer's large dogs got tired of waiting and went home.

One day the brothers came by crying. Their father and uncle were being sent to prison for stealing sinks and bathtubs from the construction site where they worked. The neighbors from across the street who were from the South said I should never have been playing with those "niggers." The Jones boys and their family moved away, and their house and trees were razed to make room for more houses.

Trick-or-treat

When Halloween and my tenth birthday came, I was told for the first time about trick-or-treating. Back home we had soaped window, tipped over outhouses and garbage cans, set water cans and anything we could think of to make life miserable for others. What was this trick-or-treat?

I should explain the water cans. Two large cans were filled with water and placed in a dark place along a sidewalk or a pathway. They were connected by a dark string. When a person walked into the string, both cans filled with water came up and covered their legs. We would hide in the bushes waiting to hear them scream.

At our new home in Seattle several friends came by and asked me to go along with them trick-or treating. What was this trick-or-treat? They told me that people were expecting us to come by and I should bring a sack to carry the loot. I took a pillow case. I dressed like a soldier, took my toy army rifle and my bag. At the first house, I said, "trick-or-treat." They gave us all a candy bar.

From then on it was more, more, more.

At dusk my friends headed home. I went on and on, as long as there was a porch light calling me. When I finally stopped, my pillow case was half full of loot. I put my candy under the bed and fed on it for several weeks.

Renton Highlands

We were able to find housing at the Highlands, which all of my school friends at Brenmar said was a tough place where people were killed every week.

The Highlands were on the mountains east of Renton overlooking Lake Washington about fifteen miles from downtown Seattle. The houses had been thrown up quickly; the area was intended as temporary housing for the duration of the war, and only war plant workers and military families were allowed to live in this community of 2,500 homes. When I visited the area sixty years later, those "temporary" buildings were still serving as homes.

We lived in a duplex not too far from the bus line and the shopping center. There was plenty of room for the four of us: a living room, two bedrooms, bathroom, a large kitchen and dining area. The front door, that we seldom used, opened into the living room, and the back door opened to the north from the kitchen onto a sidewalk leading to the store and bus stop.

Our grade school and youth center was down the hill to the west; the area recreation center was nearby the school. Wayne went there to box and learn judo, and I played basketball in the winter and baseball the rest of the year. When we visited years later, the recreation center has been restored after it had burned to the ground.

During my first week of school I kept a sharp lookout for all the killers. A boy on the playground pointed at me and then came over and asked if I were the Anderson from the Brenmar school who had broken a kid's leg in a fight on the playground. I told him that I knew nothing about anyone breaking anyone's leg. He went back and told the other boys what I had said. They all flocked around me and wanted to be my friend.   I was the killer I had been looking out for.   Needless to say I had two good years at that school.

The Japanese

No Japanese were living in the Highlands when we first arrived, but they were released from the camps shortly after we moved in. In 1942 the government had ordered the Japanese-Americans to be organized into groups and moved away from the coast. As they were allowed to return to the Seattle area, several families moved into the housing near us.

I remember an Alice Ficada and her brother Roy. I spent many days swimming and fishing with two small Japanese boys near my age. They were very clean. When I visited their house for the first time, it was empty of furniture and dishes. When asked where they slept and ate, they opened the door to a closet and showed a pile of rolled up mats. They slept on them at night and used them to sit on when they ate their meals.

When their grandmother came into the room, she surprised me because she was smaller than the boys. When we went fishing many days in Lake Washington and the Cedar River, they always caught fish. One salmon they caught was so large that when they put it over their shoulders, it dragged on the ground.

The Japanese boys were also outstanding swimmers. In the summer they took me five miles up the mountains to a crater lake where a crowd gathered to watch them dive into the deep water to retrieve coins. I held the coins for them after failing to dive to those depths. I never remember any of the Japanese who weren't glad to live in America. They too wanted to win the war.

Reportedly some saboteurs started a fire in a storage center north of the Highlands where navy flares and professional fireworks were stored. It burned for a week. We would go as close as we could get and watch as the boxes of rockets would go off. The guards made us stay back because some of the rockets would come out through the woods. Most of the trees within a block of the center had all their leaves blown off. We picked up flares and fireworks a block away after the fire was put out.

Downtown Seattle

Wayne and I would catch the Trailways bus by the shopping center early on Saturday morning and travel the fifteen miles to the penny arcades down on the Seattle waterfront. More than twenty arcades were filled with games and hand-cranked picture shows which provided fun for a crowd of boys. We would meet the same kids every week. Many Saturdays our parents both were at work, and I'm not sure they always knew where we were.

We would visit the Old Curiosity Shop before we bought our lunch and started for the movie theater. We especially admired the ugly mermaid hanging on the wall that was still there sixty years later when we went to a family reunion.

The total cost so far was about 60 cents: bus fare .10, arcades .25, lunch with drink .25; the movie with popcorn and a candy bar added .30, and the bus fare home .10. Many times we would see a Bowery Boys, western or a war picture. From the movie house we would hurry to catch the 4:00 p.m. Trailway bus.   The bus station was up the hill to the north of the theater. If we missed the bus, we would have to take the late bus and get home after dark.

The mermaid at the Old Curiosity Shop

One Saturday while my parents were at work and Wayne had gone to a camp, I decided to go to Seattle by myself. When I arrived the boys were all there. We played and then went to the show. They said goodbye and went the other way. I started for the bus station with my dime for bus fare. When I got to the top of the hill, I couldn't find my dime. I must have dropped it on the street. I hurried back down the sidewalk; the dime wasn't there.

I stood on the corner and began to cry. A lady stopped and asked if she could help. Through my tears I told her I had lost my bus fare. She put a quarter in my hand and said I would be all right. I couldn't stop crying. Someone put a dime in my hand. By the time I finished crying I had fifty-five cents.

I started for the bus station; the 4:00 p.m. bus to the Renton Highlands was just about to go. I got on and breathed a sigh of relief. I put my hand in my shirt pocket, and there was my dime. When I got home, my parents were there and wondered where I had been. When I said Seattle, they asked who I went with. I told them my story. I learned that if you cry a lot people will help you.

Good training for my years as a Salvation Army officer.

Seattle-to-Bremerton Car Ferry

From downtown Seattle you could walk onto the car ferry to Bremerton for less than a dollar. Most of the warships were dry-docked for repair at the Bremerton shipyards.

Our cousin John Anderson worked as a welder, and he invited us to come aboard one of the aircraft carriers he was working on. We went as a family, and he got us all passes to board the *Hornet* before it went back to the war in the Pacific. He had shown us a coffee can of the remains of a "Jap Zero" he had removed from the deck. Ships and sailors were everywhere. The smell of the sea mingled with burning diesel fuel and the banging of the repairs fill the air twenty-four hours seven days a week. At night employees worked under bright lights.

We boys would take the ferry just for the ride. Puget Sound was filled with warships coming and going. Sometimes on the return trip only a few people would be onboard. One day when I was eleven, I was sitting alone and found a magazine someone had left on a bench. It said "Health and Sunshine." It was my first realization what the opposite sex looked like without clothing. There was page after page of health and sunshine. I put it back on the bench and never told my mother about it.

The Seattle Times

A man came by our school and offered us free baseballs if we would sell the *Sunday Seattle Times*. He told us that we would pay seven cents for the paper and sell it for fifteen cents. We had to bring the money with us on Sunday morning to a pickup spot. I had enough for fifty papers. What a deal. He said we could sell them door to door.

Sunday morning came and at 7:30 a.m. he was there with a truckload of papers. Only five or six boys showed up to work. He gave us a big bag to put over our shoulder which held about fifty papers. I started down the street knocking on doors. I sold all my papers in an hour and a half. Some people tipped me so I earned over five dollars profit the first week.

I sold papers right up to the time we returned to Jamestown. Selling papers taught me how to show up on time, talk to people and work for my money. While the rest of the family went to the Lutheran Church in Renton, I sold papers. I could still sing the Sunday school choruses I had learned at the happy Salvation Army in Jamestown. I told my mother that I thought that the Lutheran Church had the same service every week.

I met some very strange people going door to door in the project. Many were just waking up and were only partly dressed. I would stand on the porch and wait for my money. Some were still drunk from the night before.

Beans

Most of the adults who wanted to work had jobs. The truck farmers from the Kent Washington area could not find enough workers to pick their crops. Wayne and I both went to work in the summer of 1943 picking green beans and raspberries. We could earn up to five dollars a day, which would be equivalent to sixty dollars a day now. We worked alongside Mexican families where all members worked from sunrise to sundown. The farmer paid every day.

We boys learned how to smokestack by watching how the Mexicans make three hampers of green beans out of two. When the beans were picked they would pack tightly. By pouring those from one container to another they would pack more loosely. The farmer paid us something like $1.50 a peck. We could pick three peck a day. When it came to raspberries we were paid by the quart. To make the five dollars we had to work long hours. The Mexican families were working when we came and were still working when we were boarding our bus. Wayne and I worked those fields for several summers.

Wayne and me shortly after we moved to Seattle

Drive-in Movie

The folks across the street who had told me not to play with the Jones boys were from the Deep South and spoke a new kind of English. The adults all smoked and drank a lot of beer and wine. They both worked and drove a big brown car. Their daughter who was about my age came over and wanted me to go on a date. She and I played house in her backyard. Mary Jo's mother and her boyfriend were going to a drive-in movie. They paid my way on the condition that I sit in the back seat with her. She wanted to hold my hand and tried to kiss me. I moved over and said I wanted to watch the movie. They gave me popcorn and a drink, but I never went to the movies with them again. I went back and played with the Jones boys.

Bible Camp

During our first summer in the Highlands a man came to our door and offered to take me to camp for seven dollars. There would be swimming, fishing, hiking in the woods, campfires, and good food. My mother thought it was a good idea. A friend from down the street went with me. I took my bedroll, a change of clothes and started out Monday morning to have a week of fun.

The camp had two bunkhouses and a long open shelter which served as a kitchen, dining hall and recreation hall when it rained. We sat at picnic tables and ate out of metal dishes. Hot dogs, hamburgers, macaroni and cheese and other hot dishes were served in abundance.

We played capture the flag every afternoon. What fun we had! At night we had campfires with the singing of Sunday school songs and the testimonies of some kids on how God had changed their lives. Some of the worst kids gave the best testimonies. When I asked one of the leaders how you got a testimony, he said that I had to work on one.

At night before we went to sleep, one of the leaders would come in and read *Bible* stories to us. Then he would read to us about what a Christian boy should do. He told us about the sex thing. He said that we should watch out for girls who wanted to have sex with us. No matter what they said, we should not have sex until we were married. From that time on I thought girls only wanted me for my body.

When I got home my mother asked me what I learned at camp. I said *Bible* stories and how to light a fire in the rain.

Skunk Anderson

My father Vic had earned extra money as a trapper when he was a farmer. During the depression he had worked several winters as a skinner for Porter Brothers Hide and Fur. He had been called "Skunk Anderson" by some of the family when we lived back in Jamestown. Even now Wayne gets pleasant memories of our father when he drives past a place with skunk odor in the air.

Several of my school friends wanted me to go hunting with them during the summer. We went back into the forest west of the project where the woods were full of all kinds of varmints. We made a high platform between four pine trees. We could climb up there and watch the animals pass by. I had purchased a BB gun with money earned picking beans. One of the boys had three or four spring traps. We found a place where there was a den, set our traps and anchored them to a tree. I came back by myself the next morning.

Something was moving. I pulled and pulled on the chain and finally I saw two eyes looking back at me. I jerked the trap and the skunk out came out into the open. I fired two shots from my gun. He fired back and hit his mark. I hit him with the butt of my gun. He was dead.

I ran back to where my friends lived. I pounded on the door. They called out and asked me what I wanted. I said we had caught a skunk in our trap. They said they could tell, and I was to go down and stand on the corner. They came out and we went back to find our prize and decided to bury him. That ended our desire to hunt anything else.

Mowing Lawns

I needed a job when I wasn't selling papers or picking beans. A friend suggested that we go to Renton and mow lawns. We didn't have any leads, and we didn't have a lawn mower. We got on the bus to Renton, and when we got there we started walking down the street looking for lawns that needed attention. At the first house we offered to mow her lawn for one dollar if she had a mower. She did and in a short while we had finished mowing the lawn to her satisfaction.

She said the lady across the street wanted her lawn mowed. We borrowed her lawn mower and went across the street for another dollar. We cleaned up all the clippings and trimmed the bushes. We went down the street and each earned about three dollars for our day's work. During the rainy season we mowed lawns every Saturday. I learned if you worked, you would have money.

Telephone Robbers

At the bottom of the hill to the west of the Larson's house were several new phone booths. Sometimes when we were playing nearby, I saw users pounding on the black payphones trying to get their money back. After awhile they would leave, and some bigger boys would go in the booth and come out with money. They would all get in their car and drive away. What they were doing was stuffing paper wads up the coin return and coming by with a coat hanger which they used to pull down the paper and the money.

Later we found a coat hanger and went by and took out the money before the robbers could get it. We didn't know who to give the money to, so we kept it. The older boys stopped coming when there was no change in the phones. For years I used to check the payphone coin returns. They never did catch those crooks.

The Morning Fog

There were many days when nothing could move on the road until the fog had lifted. We heard of people having to walk beside the car with a flashlight to keep the car on the road. Two thumps on the hood meant to move right, three meant to move left. One thump meant to go straight ahead. The war plants went twenty-four hours a day, seven days a week. Everyone was involved in winning the war. The fog could not slow down production. Most days it burned off by afternoon, but not always.

Boeing number one plant tried to put out a new B-17 Flying Fortress every day. We could hear them testing the engines through the fog. Then the plane would take off over the lake and fly off to the war. During our first year in the Highlands they started to make the B-29s. Where we lived there was little or no fog. It was mostly in the valleys along Puget Sound or Lake Washington.

The Perfect Model

Once a week I attended a model airplane club that met down at the end of our block. About twenty boys of varying ages attended the craft center which sold model kits and glue at cost. The leader showed us how to build a model that would fly. The frame was made from balsam wood and covered with strong silk-like paper. It was powered by a long rubber band attached to a plastic propeller which when wound up would send the plane through the air a hundred feet or so. When we put some of the smoke flares in them and sent them over the fence, the planes went down in flames.

One day while we were waiting for the leader to come, several of us boys had climbed up on the roof. The building began to shake; we screamed and held on to the chimney. We thought that a car had run into the building. The shaking lasted for over a minute. It was a small earthquake that I later found out was common. It was great fun to make these models while listening to the radio when I was home alone. No television or video games existed during those days. How did we ever survive?

The War Ended

In late April and early May of 1945 the war in Europe ended. In August the war with Japan ended after Little Boy was dropped from the Enola Gay, one of the B-29 bombers that had been built in the Renton plant.

My older brother Leonard, who had been serving in Europe, showed up at our house in the Renton Highlands. His wife Beatrice and daughter Linda stayed with us for a day or two. They slept in Wayne's and my bedroom. I remember sleeping on the floor in my parents' room for several nights and hearing strange sounds come through the wall of the apartment next door. There was a lineup to get into the bathroom in the morning.

Leonard and his family were gone in a few days. He had a job waiting for him on the railroad and a house to fix up and move into in Jamestown. Production at the war plants was being shut down. Those who had come to win the war were finding other jobs or returning home. My father's job ended and my mother's went on only for a few more weeks. My parents decided to return to Jamestown. We took our boxes of belongings, our Singer sewing machine and a new look at life back on the train and headed east to home. Many of our relations stayed in Seattle and found new jobs.

CHAPTER SEVEN

THE POST-WAR JAMESTOWN YEARS

Back to Jamestown 1946 to 1952

The war was ending; we needed to go back where our old friends and family lived--away from the sea, the mountains, the tall pines, the war workers, and the project houses row upon row. The warm winters, the indoor plumbing, the deafening sound of the planes as they went off to war, the rationing of food and gas were all coming to an end for our family.

Back in Jamestown we found that our relatives had weathered the war well. When we got off the train, Leonard was there to take us to his house with a yard filled with apple trees. It felt good to see the river again. We moved into an upstairs bedroom. I was given an army cot in my folks' room. Family and friends came by to welcome us.

There was talk about money my mother was to receive from the sale of her parents' farm, enough to buy a house and lot. My parents were old and my farther was not able to work like he had in his younger days. He went shocking wheat with some friends at a farm over by Valley City. Unemployed in Seattle after the war, he had gotten out of condition and was not able to work like he had before we moved west. Working in the hot sun, he had a slight stroke and started to use a cane.

The Granary by the Miller Store

The government was selling buildings for a reasonable price to hold grain. We purchased one and had it moved to a temporary lot next to Miller's corner grocery store on highway 281 and 2nd

Avenue NW. Windows and doors were put in, and a loft door and a foldaway stairway were also added to make the upstairs available for bedrooms.

In several months the house was moved across the river to a lot on 2nd Avenue NW where we had space for a garden, well and outhouse. The house was remodeled and expanded by us three sons during the next six years. Wayne and I lived there through the passing of our parents. The title for the house was put in Leonard's name when my mother became ill.

After her death Leonard paid the funeral bills and in a few years sold the house. Wayne and I had moved away to our new lives.

Who is this New Kid?

When school started, not many of the other kids knew who I was. I dressed like the kids in Seattle, a flight jacket, a black stocking hat, and my hair was combed back. I walked and talked like a sailor. When I gave my name they said, "You're not the Lester Anderson who used to live here?" I said I was. Some of the kids from the Washington grade school said they remembered me. I was welcomed and made new friends every day. Red Perry showed up and introduced me to all his friends. I belonged.

They made me captain of a seventh grade basketball team. I got a bicycle to ride to school. I joined the art club and soon became known as one who could draw pictures. I made a poster for the Veterans of Foreign Wars Poppy Day and received a second prize of two dollars.. For the next five years I won the first prize of five dollars in this poster contest. The first year I sat and watched the adult-only films of the Jewish death camps while I waited for my prize. I don't think that those army films have ever been shown to the American public.

Cold, Cold Winter

Every Sunday we drove out in the country to visit our relatives and have dinner. School took up much of my time. October came with a city wide Halloween costume parade that ended at the city auditorium. We were tricking not looking for treats. I remember the river had already frozen over even though there was no snow. It got colder each day; by November it was freezing every day. We needed stocking hats, gloves, scarves, overshoes, long winter underwear and heavy coats. The oil heater at our house ran day and night. You could see your breath most of the day. I got a pair of ice skates and a hockey stick and joined the other boys on the river ice.

Thanksgiving came and relatives were everywhere. Next came Christmas which we celebrated at Leonard's house. I remember Linda, my niece, and her," Is that all there is?" as she sat in a pile of presents and wrapping paper. I remembered those warm winters in Seattle. Wayne came home from Spokane where he had been going to high school while living with Gladys and Ove who had moved there at the end of the war.

As that first winter wore on, the evening darkness came sooner and the morning daylight came later. It was dark by 4:30 in the afternoon and still dark at 8:30 in the morning. Many nights as I walked home in the bright moonlight, I could hear the ice cracking in the river. Most winters the ice in the river froze to thirty-four inches.

By the end of October we would be out skating on black ice, ice without snow. We could look down through the ice and see the fish swimming by. River ice was always dangerous because the muskrats and beaver would make air holes; when snow covered the ice you would see them only as dark spots which let you know of the danger. High winds and temperatures of forty below made it dangerous to be outside any length of time.

The Big Fight

Wayne was trained as a boxer while we lived in the Renton Highlands project. He entered a Golden Glove Boxing match at the city armory. When we got there it was packed to the rafters. Everything was in place. The ring looked like it was for professionals, and many matches were planned for the night. I went downstairs with Wayne where they taped his hands and fitted him with the proper gloves. They asked him if he had ever fought in a ring before. He was going to be fighting one of the best fighters in his weight class. When they announced his match, he and the coach went up the stairs to the ring. I stayed behind to take care of his clothes.

As I got to the top of the stairs, I heard the crowd give a great roar and a clanging of the bell; they were taking someone out of the ring. It wasn't Wayne--it was some other guy. It was a TKO. They had called the fight after one minute.

Some time later I had been stopped in the park on my way home by five members of the notorious "Darby Gang." They were going to "de-pants" me as they had other boys. It happened that Wayne came by while they were holding me down. He said he would fight any one of them one at a time starting with Darby. They talked with each other for a minute, and then let me go. They never stopped me again.

Valentine's Day Party

Red, Bob and Allen were all going to a party at the "armory." Red said, "No, no, not the 'armory,' the 'army.'" I asked what army? He said, "The Salvation Army--they got majors, captains and girls." When it was getting dark, we went to the basement hall. As we went in, I remembered it was the same place where Wayne had won the checkers contest.

The hall was filled. All the good looking girls from the seventh grade were there. A Captain Walter Handsome was in charge. He could play the piano and made the party real fun. We played games where we held hands with the girls while we danced around in circles.

All the teens made me feel welcome. They invited me back to their Sunday school. Red and some of the girls lived in my part of town so we walked home together. Charlotte, who was one of the girls I remembered from Washington grade school, walked with us part of the way. Cleo and Laverne, who lived across the field from our new house, also invited me to come to church.

A New Salvation Army

Red came by to make sure I got to Sunday school. It was February of 1947 and I was fourteen years old. The hall was filled. A brass band was playing with four or five of the teenagers playing shiny horns. The songs were happy like the ones I remembered from before. The Captain played a great piano while everyone clapped along with the singing. Nine of the best looking seventh grade girls were there.

The Captain welcomed me and later asked if I wanted to join the band. I said I didn't have a horn and didn't know how to play one. He said to come back next week and he would teach me during the beginners' band practice on Wednesday.

Seven or eight teenagers and three adults were there that night. He taught us how to make a tone with the mouthpiece and gave me a book to study. I liked this place. They liked me. I attended all the meetings. In a month I had a cornet and was playing the easy tunes. The captain had a party for the youth every other week.

I was walking home with the girls two or three nights a week. We became good friends. I joined the *Bible* class for corps cadets so I began to understand what it was to be a Christian. I was moved to the bass horn, which was easier, and I was given a part to play by myself. We went to rallies in Fargo and Valley City with great crowds of kids coming from all over North Dakota. We went to band camp north of Minneapolis at the Salvation Army Silver Lake Camp.

Play Ball

In the spring of 1946 I went out for the Northwest Junior High baseball team. About twenty boys showed up for tryouts at Bollinger Field. I had not played the year before. I sat on the bench until every one else had been tested. They asked me what position I played. I said I played third base and pitched some times. They told me to try pitching to some of their best batters. I went to the mound and did what the coach in Seattle had told me to do. I threw three strikes across the plate. They said I should try it again. When I finished they said they had their pitcher for this year. We won our first three games.

When we got way ahead in the game, I would go over and play third base. When I left to work at the Salvation Army camp, I led the league in pitching and was second in hitting. When I returned in the fall, they said I had led the league all summer. I didn't know anything about those standings.

It was time to play flag football. I played on the Northwest team and got my first black eye which lasted for three weeks. I was in with all the good players. My uncle Lee brought my mother by in his car to see me play while I was on third base. When he was in his nineties, he told me of this event and that I had muffed a grounder. He was a great player and had been a coach for years.

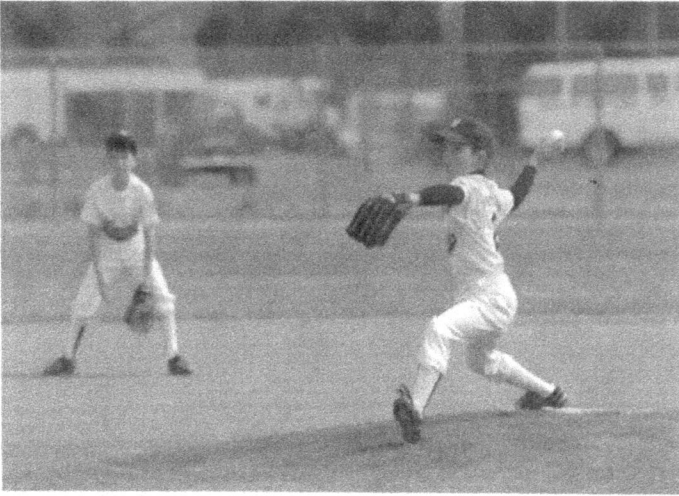

Would You Like a Job?

The captain announced that there was an opening at the Salvation Army Camp. I told him I would take the job that paid five dollars a week with room and board. When I told my mother, she said it was OK but asked where the camp was. I told her it was near Minneapolis and that I could work for ten weeks. She wanted to know who was going to wash my clothes. The Captain had told me that they had a lady who would do my laundry.

When the other campers from Jamestown left music camp for home, they told me it was time to go to work. I was assigned as pot and pan boy for the St. Paul side of the camp. They gave me a bed in a cabin with two older staff boys from Fargo. I liked the food and the job. When I wasn't working, I was out in a boat fishing or down at the dock swimming.

We had programs every night and played baseball with the family campers in the afternoon. The second cook's son, Art, and I became good friends. The whole thing was a class act: three camps would have joint staff parties and a big corps meeting every Sunday evening. So I learned what the real Army was all about. I returned to work at this camp three more summers. My first assignment as an officer was as program director at the Minneapolis camp.

Moving Along

When I returned home after the first year at camp, everything had changed. My father was not well. I took some of the money I had saved and bought a new red bike. The first night I had it, I parked it next to our wood box by our front door. In the morning it was gone. The police told me there was no hope of finding it.

I played in the band and took part in everything at the Army. In the cold winter months the Captain would take the teenagers on a "Tramp," as he called it, through the woods. We would walk through the snow for miles and end up at the Army hall for lunch and hot cocoa. We thought he was the greatest guy on earth. The teenagers who went to the Sunday night meetings would go from there to the Grand Theater. We would pool our money to buy a ticket for one of the girls, who would go up to the balcony and let the rest of us in.

Captain Handsome started a radio program with the theme song, "Salvation Army, Army of God." When the school asked me what church I belonged to, I put down, "Salvation Army." Many of the teens who I knew were proud to be part of the Army.

I Needed a Job

When I went into the eighth grade, I needed a job for the winter months. I went from store to store; no one was hiring. The Red Owl grocery store, which had moved south of the post office, needed a boy in the meat department. They paid thirty-five cents an hour and said I could work two hours weekdays and eight hours on Saturday. I became a boner, hamburger maker, chicken chopper and a steakette tenderizer. Later they moved me to the produce department. I also had to work as a box boy when needed. We used boxes to carry the groceries out to the car. There were no shopping carts as there are today.

I worked there until I was a junior; they raised my pay to fifty cents an hour. I had to wear a white shirt and a red bow tie. I got the white shirt from Old Nick at the Salvation Army for twenty-five cents and the bow tie from Penny's for a dollar. Wayne had a winter job at the Farmers Union cooperative store known as the Equity Creamery where he was paid seventy-five cents an hour. I used some of my money to pay for my own school lunch which was a dollar twenty-five a week.

One day in the fall they made some staff changes. The manager of the produce department was going to be made general store manager. He had been an alcoholic who had become a Jehovah's Witness. He knew I was in the Salvation Army and that I preached in the street meetings. He called a staff meeting of about twenty-five people. He said he had taken this job for one reason; he wanted to fire one person he just couldn't tolerate. He pointed at me and said, "Anderson, you're fired."

I needed the eight dollars a week to live on. What to do? I walked down to where Wayne worked and told, Hank, his boss, that I had been fired. He said he needed another man and would pay me seventy-five cents an hour. That was twelve dollars a week to me. God was still taking care of me. I worked there until I moved out west for the summer.

Some Changes Were Made

After my second summer at the Salvation Army Camp by Minneapolis, I returned home to find that the Salvation Army had changed. Captain Handsome had been in jail for having a sexual tryst with one of the girls in the band. All charges had been dropped by the family of the girl, so he and his family moved back to Minneapolis. All but three of the teenage girls in the corps were gone. A retired lady Major was in charge. The meetings had dropped in half in attendance. Most of the old people were still there. No one would tell me exactly what had happened.

A tall Major who played a guitar and sang in a baritone voice arrived from Bismarck where he had been the corps officer. Major Walter Lee with his housekeeper, Nuebe, and her crippled daughter, Silvia, moved into the upstairs apartment. Every Sunday he had a printed program with a new song or choruses he had written the week before. I was fifteen when he arrived. He never spoke of the Captain or the thirteen-year-old girl who was involved with him. More people started to come to the corps. My father had gotten worse; his memory was totally gone and he was in the hospital.

The Four-Door with a Stick Shift

My brother, Wayne, who was working in construction at that time, came home with a 1929 Plymouth four-door with a stick shift. After the war cars were hard to come by. This was the best he could do at the time. It needed a paint job so we got a can of blue metal paint and two brushes, and after several days we had a shiny car parked in our front yard. It was the old style with a box-like look.

It had a floor shift that would jump out of high gear, so we used a stick with a notch in it to hold it in place. The windshield was straight up and down. There were side window air vents that opened to let in the cool air as you whipped down the highway at thirty-five miles an hour. If you needed a part or a tire, you went out to the junkyard, and for a dollar or two you were on your way.

One day we decided to go out in the country for a swim. We went out highway 10 west until we found a gravel pit with clean clear water on the south side of the road. We parked the car and jumped in. The water was cold and deep with a mud bottom. The second time we decided to dive in. When Wayne came up out of the water, his glasses were gone. He was blind without his glasses. I could not drive yet. We sat on the bank trying to think of a way to get back to town.

I remembered how the Japanese boys would dive for coins. I

dove in the water and went way down into the mud bottom. My outstretched hand caught something that felt like a stick. When I came to the surface through a cloud of muddy water, there were his glasses caught between my fingers

We rejoiced and drove back to town. Later that week Wayne took me out in the country for driving lessons. In the winter when the temperature got down below zero, we would put rags soaked in kerosene in a coffee can, light it and push it under the crankcase. Most of the time we could get the car started. After a year or so Wayne bought a blue '39 Ford which he drove until 1952. In the fall of 1951 Wayne purchased a 1941 Nash for me for a hundred twenty-five dollars with money I had earned working for Woody's Silo Company.

Woody's Silo Company

The Wensel brothers from Beulah, North Dakota, attended Jamestown College and worked summers for Woody. In the summer of 1951 I needed a job that paid more than five dollars a week. I asked around and there were no job openings. Someone said the only place that needed help was Woody's Silo Company. They paid well but the work was heavy and dangerous.

I asked and they said they needed an outside man to work with the Wensels. The job that was open paid thirty-five dollars for each silo constructed. They planned to put up three silos a week for ten weeks. Meals and lodging were provided by the farmers. They told me I needed boots and work gloves. They came by in a black Ford flatbed truck loader with equipment. I sat in the cab between the brothers. They were full of fun and were glad to have me as part of their team.

We drove west toward Bismarck. They said we had to start work by noon. When we got to the first farm, we unloaded and they began to show me what to do. All the materials had been delivered earlier and the slab had been put in next to the barn. We had to put up the silo and finish the job. They explained that we would put up a ring of staves and hold them together with metal straps. They worked on the inside and I worked on the outside. I would send up the staves with a gas driven wrench as they went higher and higher. The operation looked safe and easy.

The staves weighed sixty pounds each and the window frames weighed one hundred twenty pounds. By the time we finished for the day, they were up forty feet in the air. They had scaffolding that was jacked up by adding extensions of pipe. They walked on boards that were held up by wings on the scaffolding.

They told me in the morning that it was time to straighten and tighten the straps. It took a hammer to straighten out the straps and two wrenches to tighten the bolts. They dropped down a block and tackle with a hook on it and told me to hook it to the swing chair. The rope at the top was hooked to a clamp that was placed over one of the staves. I began to pull myself up strap after strap until I was thirty feet off the ground.

A silo is round with no place to hang on. By the end of the summer I could work to the top, climb over the edge and move the clamp from side to side. I learned to wear a construction helmet because they dropped hammers and other things from the top all the time. We built over twenty silos in western North Dakota that summer. The next summer when I was on the west coast, they called and wanted me to come back to work. They said that the man who had my job had fallen and died on the job. I never went back. God had protected me again.

The Spike Pitcher

During the late summer of 1947 I was offered a few days' work on Dave Lovan's farm north of where we lived. I told my family about my job helping with the harvest; all they said was to make sure that I didn't get the job of the "spike pitcher." When I showed up at daybreak they told me I would get fifty cents an hour and we would be working two days.

The thrashing machine was hooked up to a running tractor, and the horse-drawn hay wagons were out in the field loading shocks of grain. Two men were on a wagon and several men with pitchforks were loading the shocks onto the wagons. The grain would go from the thrashing machine to a wagon and the straw would be blown out into a pile. When the straw pile got too big, they would move the thrashing machine to another spot.

About twenty men were working the field. The straw boss told me I should take a pitchfork and get on the wagons as they came in. My job was to help throw the shocks into the hopper as each team came in to unload. I thought I had the best job of all.

We went to the farmhouse for lunch. Twenty men and boys sat at one table. So much food, all the fried chicken you could eat with pies and cakes, bread and butter. We went back to work. I liked my job. The wagons kept coming. In the afternoon they brought out some lunch and lemonade. About six they called us to eat again. More food. At dusk they shut down and said we would start a six the next morning. When I got home they asked me what job I had. I told them how much fun I was having throwing the bundles into the thrashing machine. They said I was the "spike pitcher." I made ten dollars for my two days' work.

To Sail or Not to Sail

Several friends and I had decided we wanted to build a boat. We found the plans for a small canvas covered sailboat. We studied the plans and decided to build in my brother Leonard's garage. We cut the struts and all the other parts from lumber we scrounged from our yards. We picked up other parts from the garage and the hardware store. After several weeks we had the shell of the boat.

We needed the canvas which we located covering a cement mixer at a construction site on Bollinger field. We nailed it to the frame, covered it with tar, painted it blue and put it in the river to see if it would float. It floated. Two of us rowed it up and down the river. It had a rudder, keel, mast, front and back and a sail that we made from several old sheets.

We carried it all the way to Long Slough. We put up the twelve-foot mast, connected the sail and tacked our way to the north end of the slough. We were sailors for several weeks sailing the half-mile-long lake with ease. We would hide our boat in a low hanging grove of trees so it could not be seen from the bank. One day when we came to sail it, the boat was gone. We looked along the shore on both sides and finally found it shot full of holes and broken so it couldn't be repaired. We moved on.

The Ice Man

Allen Benson and I had gone hunting early one winter evening. We walked north on the James River a mile or so and then crossed through the woods to the north end of Long Slough. We were walking home in the moonlight. The slough at that time was filled with muskrats and beaver. The ice was covered with snow and the temperature was beginning to drop. I was telling Allen about the air holes made by the muskrats. I said you could only see them as a dark spot in the snow. We were both carrying guns.

We were in the middle of the lake when Allen disappeared into the snow. He popped up like a cork. I grabbed his hand and pulled him back up on the ice. He picked up his gun and we kept walking. His clothes began to freeze. We hurried to the road. There were lights on at the Lovan's house. They let us in and helped Allen take off his frozen clothing. Mrs. Lovan got some of her husband's things for him to wear home. They covered him with blankets and put his feet in cold water. In an hour we were on our way home.

Day of the Gun

Wayne and I had both been shooting .22 rifles since we were young. We bought a bolt action Mossburger with a clip for about fourteen dollars, which I used to go hunting in the north woods between Long Slough and the James River. When we first returned from the West, a group of boys from the neighborhood would camp out at the Old Boy Scout camp. We would hunt crows, rabbits and anything else that moved. We stayed in tents and brought enough food for a day or two. I remember the day we ran out of everything but beans and pancake syrup. We went hunting for frogs with no success and packed up and walked home.

When I went into the 10th grade, I met Marion and Byron, whose father worked installing car radios and had his own ham radio station. The two boys were crude in some ways but liked to hunt. We had great fun together. One Saturday in 1950 we decided to go out shooting by the dam construction site. We were shooting at anything that moved when we saw a white box in the distance along the river that said "DANGER" in bright red letters. We shot at it but nothing happened.

When we walked over to look inside, we thought it would be empty but it was half full of dynamite sticks. The lock had been broken; someone had taken some sticks because there was a trail of sticks that led off into the woods. I explained to the boys that it took a cap to make the dynamite explode. I demonstrated by banging two sticks together.

We each took several sticks which we put in the pockets of our khaki army jackets. We walked our usual trails and ended up on the hillside next to the gravel road we took home. We had only one stick left which we leaned against a tree. We sat and emptied our guns into the stick. I was so smart, nothing had happened. We walked to the top of the hill where we were about a quarter of a block away from the stick. Byron turned and said he would take one more shot. We could just see the stick in the distance. He shot and the stick exploded. The bark flew off the tree, dust filled the air, and the ground shook. We all lost our hearing for a few minutes--we were all shaking. God knew how to teach a lesson without killing us.

When I got home my mother was out hanging clothes on the line. She asked if I had heard the explosion. She didn't think they were working on the dam on Saturdays. I never told her.

The Day of the Frog

When we boys would go camping at the old Boy Scout camp, we would fill our water canteens at a spring. It was located on the side of the hill about a half mile south of the camp. The water came out very cold and crystal clear. We were lucky. Someone before us had installed a ten-foot-three-inch pipe back into the spring.

One morning we came to fill our canteens and found the water had stopped coming. We pulled the pipe out and discovered that it was plugged. It looked like someone had put rocks or gravel in the pipe. We shook it, and shook it again. Out came one frog. We looked in again. It was still blocked. We shook it with all our might. Out came another and another until we counted twenty-two frogs on the ground. We were drinking frog water all the time and didn't know it. Next time we came we cleaned out the pipe before we ever drank there again. That spring still flows to this day.

A Donkey Trail

A man named Holder owned a herd of donkeys that he used in the summer for donkey baseball. He kept them in a large wooded field several miles north of Lovan's farm. He had a small house in the woods by the river. Sometime he would leave the door unlocked and we would go inside when it rained. In the fall the donkeys would let us ride them. They were all trained differently. Some would run a short distance and then put their heads down making the rider slide off. Some would run and then try to buck you off. We fashioned a bridle and rode them bareback.

One day we came and there were only three donkeys. There were fences so they couldn't get out of the field and the woods. We were able to catch the donkeys and ride them without bridles. They took us down along the river and up a steep hill; they went down a cow path through the trees and tried to brush us off.

They came to a slate bank that ran down to the river; they turned and went down the bank. We thought we were going into the water. At the bottom of the slate was a trail that led along the river to a small hill. On the other side of the hill were all the other donkeys. We walked back to where we had left our guns. Holder moved out to Hollywood where he opened a wild animal farm which was used by most motion pictures studios during the 60s and 70s. We rode the donkeys for several more years.

CHAPTER EIGHT

I MAKE A COMMITMENT

New Year's Eve 1948

It was a very cold night. The Watch Night Service which started at 9:00 p.m. at the Salvation Army was well attended with Major Walter Lee at his best. A Commandant Wiggins was the guest speaker. Several new teenage boys from the west coast had come to the meeting. The girls had all gone to talk to them. I sat alone on the back row. Time came for the lunch and fellowship in the basement hall.

I put on my blue topcoat and decided I would go home and get some money to go to the midnight movie at the Grand Theater. I thought it might be a good time for me to give this Salvation Army thing up. I hurried home through the park to my house. The lights were on. They asked why I was home so early. I said I had decided to go to the midnight movie. I got my fifty-cent piece and started for the theater.

It was getting colder. As I came down Main Street I could see that the line for the movie was long. I got on the end and stood for a while in the cold. I was deciding to quit the Army and find something else to do with all my time. There were other girls and I could find God in a lot of other churches. The theater was letting people in. The line began to move. I was cold. I looked for my fifty cents--it was gone. There was a hole in my topcoat pocket. I was too cold to walk home. What should I do? Everything was closed. I knew that the Army Hall was still open. I walked the two blocks to the hall and went in and up the front stairs. They were just starting the last meeting. They didn't know that I had been gone. I sat back down in the same chair I had been sitting in.   The Chapel was warm.   The preacher was giving a simple message. I was still going to quit. At the end they were giving an altar call for people to come up and get saved. I was ready to go. I bowed my head for the prayer.

Someone put a hand on my shoulder and said it was time for me to get right with God. It was Dan Burks, one of the boys from the West. He offered to go forward and pray with me. He opened his *Bible* and read John 3:16 replacing the word, "world" with my name. For the first time it made sense to me. I was a sinner who needed to get saved and born again. I asked God to forgive me for everything that I had ever done wrong. A peace came over me I had never had before. I was new from the inside out. The guilt was gone. Everyone congratulated me for my decision. The Major said he would have a special prayer for me.

I walked home with the girls and it was as if my feet never touched the ground. The wind had stopped blowing and a bright moon lit our way home. I went to bed and thanked God for his forgiveness. I was a new person. When I was putting my topcoat away, I found the fifty-cent piece in the lining of the coat.

A Gray Uniform

The next day at school no one noticed that I was changed. I felt as if God were with me. I was happy. After work I went down to the hall to see what was going on. There seemed to be a meeting every night. I stopped going to shows. I started to read the *Bible* every day. Major Lee gave me several books by the Salvation Army on how to be a soldier. He asked me if I would like one of his old uniforms that he would put soldier's trim on. I was now six-foot tall and weighed about 150 pounds. The uniform fit me like it was made for me. It had a high collar so I could wear it with a tee shirt. I wore it on Sundays.

He also gave me a Sunday school class to teach. When I asked who was in the class, he said boys from six to ten years old. I had to find the boys and bring them to Sunday school. They ended up being as follows: Brian Haines, Dewayne, Clarence, and Bobby

Elsted, Bobby Glowax, Gene Talken and several of his little brothers. Every Sunday there were eight to ten boys in my class. We would go on hikes on Saturday and I would go by and pick them up on Sunday.

Sixteen Years Old in 1948

I came home one afternoon from school, and my mother told me that my father, who had been bedridden in the hospital as a result of strokes, had died. She told me that it was too bad that I never really got to know my father during his best days. He was buried from a Lutheran Church with the Reverend N. E. McCoy giving the message. My father told me when I was young that he only gave money to the Salvation Army and the Reverend McCoy.

Months later I came home to find a Mr. Sigger Dahl and my mother drinking coffee at the kitchen table. I sat on the couch and read my Army book while I listened. He was talking to her about going away. She told him that she had her house, garden and her two boys to take care of. Several hours later he left never to return. He was someone from her distant past I was getting more interested in the Salvation Army. Major Lee and the other soldiers were very kind during this time.

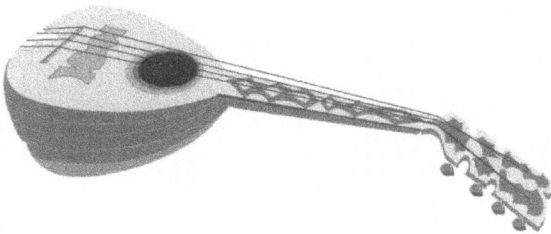

A Mandolin

Workers were cleaning out some cabinets in the band room and came across an old bowl type mandolin. They asked me if I wanted it. I took it and bought strings at the music store. No matter how I tried I could not get it to make music. One of the Home League ladies had a son whom I had gone to school with that played a mandolin. I went by to visit Viral Berndt who lived in a little trailer with his older brother and mother behind the National Tea store. He got out his mandolin and played the tune, "Little Brown Jug." He showed me how to tune it and taught me a few cords.

Once I had it tuned I learned how to play the scales. I learned to read music and played for hours. I have been playing for the last fifty years, sometimes before as many as three hundred people. I purchased my first modern mandolin from Sears for thirty-five dollars.. The one I now play is electrified and has been refitted by a skilled finisher from the Gibson Mandolin company. I use it for sing-a-longs in Sunday school and church. I have played in several Salvation Army string bands.

The Open Air Meetings (Street Meetings)

Major Lee wanted the band to play three nights a week down on Main Street by the Blackstone Hotel next to the White Drug store. On Tuesday, Thursday and Sunday evening six or seven band members and three or four soldiers would conduct a half-hour evangelistic service. Sometimes we would have a large crowd listening.

The first time that the Major asked me to give my testimony, I quoted John 3:16 and said I was a new Christian. Later he asked me to give a short message and I spoke about the "Days of Noah." Old Nick Wagner beat the big bass drum so people could hear it blocks away even when they couldn't hear the band or the message. Sometimes I would see some of the kids from school pass by or stand around the corner and listen to me give my

message and testimony

When I was in the tenth grade the members of the football team began calling me, "Boom, Boom Anderson." In chorus they would sing, "Salvation Army, Army of God" in remembrance of Captain Handsome whom they spoke of often. They wanted to know if I was doing the girls at the Army the way he had. I told them I didn't understand what they were talking about. I had to play hard to make the team.

I Made the Team

I liked team sports. In the summer it was baseball, in the fall it was football, in the winter it was basketball, and in the spring it was volleyball. I played varsity football for three years as a right end. My number was "67"and I traveled all over North Dakota with the team. As a senior I started every game for the Jamestown Blue Jays.

When I was in the tenth grade, I returned home late from camp. Practice had already started. I came into the locker room which was small for 65 boys. I got my pads, helmet, shoes and other equipment and looked for a place to sit down. There was an open bench in the middle of the room. There were pads on both ends with an empty space between them. I asked if I could sit there. Those in the room said it would be OK. I went to take my shower.

I heard yelling coming from the locker room. Two of the loud voices wanted to know who had the nerve to sit on their bench. I came from the shower. There were the two stars of the team. They said, "Is that stuff yours, Anderson?" There was a hush that fell over the crowd. They wanted to see who would kill me first. In a small voice I said, "Yes, it's mine." They looked at each other and said, "That would be just fine." I spent the rest of the year sitting between the two stars. I knew God was watching over me.

They both went on to play for big league colleges. Jerry played for Northwestern as their fullback, and Charles played for Alabama in the Gator Bowl. I wasn't good but I worked hard at being a Christian and doing my best.

I made the basketball team as a freshman, but failed to read the second list and went out and got a job. When they came to me and asked why I didn't show up for practice, I said my name wasn't on the list. They said I had missed the second list. I went on to play intramural basketball for three years. I was the captain of the losing team in the championship game. I was the captain of the winning volleyball team. Baseball was in the summer when I was away working.

The Hammer

Mr. Hammer was a good teacher. Among other things he was in charge of the intramural basketball league for boys. He didn't come to all the games, but he knew who I was and for some reason didn't seem to like me. I had done well in his mechanical drawing class. I think he didn't like my Salvation Army association. During the championship game he had changed the rules to make four seven-minute quarters with no time-outs. The clock even ran while the free throws were being shot. At the end of the game we were three points behind. The other team stood and argued as to who should shoot the technical foul free throw. I called time-out and he charged me with another technical foul. We were going to lose.

I stood in the center circle while they argued as to who would shoot those shots and the clock ran out. I removed my soaking wet game shirt, and without looking I threw it on the stage as I had done as a regular team player. It sailed through the air, and just as Mr. Hammer was turning to see the final shot, it hit him in the face. He was fifty feet away. I could not have done that again if I tried a hundred times. I couldn't help but grin. That was it. I started for the shower room; he came down the steps from the stage and told me that would cost me three nights of detention. I told him I was sorry and that it was an accident. He stomped off.

My team came down to where I was and were ready to beat him up for letting the other team cheat us out of the game. I told them to do nothing or it would cost me. They quieted down and left. I stayed behind and cleaned up the shower room. When I came to the door to go out, Hammer and a crowd of boys were there. He called me by name and said he was going to take back the three hours of detentions. Before I could thank him, he slammed me with, "I am going to expel you for three days!"

I tried to get him to change his mind. He told the office that if they didn't expel me he would quit. Here I was a big Christian going off to be a Salvation Army officer in several months. My mother was in the hospital dying from cancer. Someone had stolen my last three pairs of tennis shoes and two pair of overshoes in the last month from my locker. Now this is what I would call a bad day.

I went to work and told the boss that I had been expelled for the next three days. He said, "I need you to come to work during the day for the rest of the week."

At noon on Wednesday I thought I would sneak into the lunch line. I had paid for the week's meal in advance. I came quietly in the back door and down the stairs. As I rounded the corner someone said, "He's here." They said they wanted me up front.

As I walked along they began to cheer. When I reached the front of the line 150 students were cheering. For the next two days and the rest of the year I was a hero. Some teachers stopped me in the hall and told me they were on my side. The high school newspaper student staff changed their last edition with articles that inferred that the administration was spineless. They had given a dummy copy to their advisor. After she had reviewed it, they switched the copy.

I sent a Christmas card to Hammer for the next three years.

Mr. Intramural Basketball

The Week My Mother Died

It was graduation time. I had visited my mother in the Jamestown hospital almost every day since March. I kept my mandolin in the closet next to her bed; I would sing a little church song. I remember one day there was a man down the hallway screaming. When I asked the nurse what the problem was, she told me that he was dying from the same thing my mother had. He just wasn't ready to die. I talked to my mother even when she seemed to be sleeping. The last day I sang and said goodbye it was the week of graduation. They told my sister Gladys when she came up later that day that she had died in her sleep.

She was buried from the same church as my father with the Reverend McCoy and the Reverend Johnson from the Lutheran Church taking part in the service. I sang as a solo one of the songs I had sung to my mother in the hospital, "There's a Land that is Fairer than Day." Wayne had graduated from Jamestown College and I from high school. Our mother knew that we had graduated.

When the funeral was over, we started to pack to leave with Gladys and Loren for Pasco, Washington, in Wayne's '39 blue Ford. We drove the entire way with few stops. As we were coming down the mountains, Wayne was asleep in the back seat. When we started down the narrow road, the big trucks were coming and going by us. We rounded a curve and could see the rooftops of a city far below. Wayne awoke looked out the window and screamed. He wanted to know why he wasn't the one driving on these dangerous roads. He didn't fall asleep again until we got to Pasco.

My graduation picture from Jamestown High School

CHAPTER NINE

MY EARLY YEARS IN THE SALVATION ARMY

People and Events of Interest 1952-62

The Tri-Cities

After our mother's death in May of 1952 Wayne and I went west to live with our sister Gladys Larson in Pasco, Washington, for the summer. Her husband Ove was a barber with his own shop. Their son Loren was nine years old and liked to play basketball in their driveway next to an apricot tree. The cities of Pasco, Kennewick and Richland made up the tri-cities. The Larsons had a basement bedroom where we could stay while we looked for work. Wayne found a job driving truck in the wheat harvest.

I went from store to store looking for a summer job, but no one wanted a temporary worker. I told them that I planned to go to the Salvation Army School in the fall to become an officer. The Washington Hardware in Kennewick was not going to hire me until the owner heard me say Salvation Army. He came out of his office and said I could work for ten weeks at fifty dollars a week. I went to work the next Monday.

He told me he wanted me to talk with a lawyer friend down the street who had been an officer in the Salvation Army where he had led the city youth brass band. The attorney told me the sad story of how headquarters would not let him go to the funeral of his girlfriend, so he quit and moved back home. He said that was thirty years ago and many times he wished he had stayed. I saw him only one more time. One of the men from the appliance department who lived in Pasco picked me up for work every morning at 7:30 a.m. down at the corner from my sister's house.

They moved me from department to department. I sold pots and pans, hardware, paint, and fishing equipment. I learned to cut glass, rope, chain, copper tubing, and pipe. I put together lawnmowers, wheelbarrows, wagons, tricycles and bicycles.

One day while putting a bicycle together in the basement, I was humming the tune to "Amazing Grace." One of the workers came down the stairs and asked me if I were a Christian. I told her I was and that I was going to be an officer in the Salvation Army.

She said they needed a nice young man in their church. One of the young ladies in their church was dating a wild boy whom they did not approve of. She said if I wanted to come to their Nazarene church, they would pick me up on Sunday morning. She said the boy's name was "Wayne Bouder" and that I should look out for him.

The church building was small but well attended. They introduced me to the young lady whose father owned the Nash and Hudson dealership. After the morning service they invited me to their lovely home for dinner where I sat next to their daughter. Some of the church members who had been Salvationists took me around to tell about the Salvation Army. I wore my uniform, played my mandolin and sang Army songs. At the end of the summer the church offered to pay my way through their college in Idaho. I told them that God had called me to be an officer and I must go to Chicago.

I attended the Sunday evening youth meeting where I met many great teens and young adults. Among them was Wayne Bouder, who drove a green Chevrolet and looked a little like the "Fonz." We became good friends after I told him how they wanted me to take away his girlfriend, and we spent all summer doing things together. He picked me up for church and took me home from work most days. When I was in need of money to go home at Christmas time from the Chicago Training College he sent me a ten dollar money order.

From Pasco to Chicago

The bus ride from Pasco to Jamestown took two days with stops at many small towns until we got to Spokane; from there I changed to the express bus with only about five stops. I had about $200 left when I got to my brother Leonard's house. The new corps officers, Captain and Mrs. Leslie Chase, and their family of five welcomed me. At my corps farewell meeting the captain said he would be taking me to Minneapolis for the divisional farewell meeting.

At that meeting they took up an offering which gave me another ninety dollars, but by the time I paid for my uniform, *Bible* and entrance fee I was down to less than ten dollars. They told me that I needed at least two dollars a week for personal items.

They would have sent me home but I told them I didn't have a home to go to, so they kept me. Every week from then on, there was an envelope in my mailbox with two dollars from an unknown friend.

The Heralds Session

There were forty cadets in the "Heralds" session. While I was studying in the library, some of the girl cadets made it a practice to come by and run their fingers through my hair. A cadet named Laura, who often did the hair bit, asked me if I had a girlfriend. I told her I did but she was far away. She said she knew of a perfect girl for me who lived in Wisconsin, "Betty Chapin, " who would be attending the Training College the next year. I was commissioned in the spring of 1953 as a probationary Lieutenant along with thirty-eight other cadets.

Madison Avenue 'Tom'

During the first month at the school all the cadets went downtown to the historic Chicago Temple Corps for a Friday night meeting. The cadets conducted several street meetings out on Madison Avenue where I had the opportunity to pray with several men at the drum head. When the street meeting finished, the cadets and officers returned to the Temple Corps. Several of the men wanted to know where they could spend the night. Someone told me that there were beds at the Harbor Light Corps which was just down the street. I started walking with the men to where they would be taken care of for the night.

It ended up being over ten blocks away. Both sides of the street were filled with crowds of people; some lying dead drunk on the street, some sleeping in the doorways. Down the alley you could see groups of men sharing a bottle from a paper sack. The bar doors were open, filling the air with smoke, loud music and the smell of cheap booze.

By the time I got to the Harbor Light I had gathered a group of about twenty men who wanted me to get them inside for the night. I knocked on the door. The man who opened the door said they were filled and had no more room. The man named Tom, with matted hair and clothes soaked in wine and human waste whom I had prayed with at the meeting, was known to him and would never be allowed back in because he was a troublemaker. I told the man that he had gotten saved and would be a changed man. He smiled and closed the door.

I left the men standing in the cold night by the door and walked back to the Temple Corps, arriving there just in time to catch the bus back to the training college. Some of the cadets asked where I had been. When I told them, they said I had a lot to learn.

Three months later I was part of a brigade of cadets who were doing the Sunday morning meeting at the Chicago south side adult rehabilitation center. At the end of the meeting I was shaking the hands of the men as they passed by on their way to the dining room. They were all dressed in suits with white shirts and ties, their hair combed and their shoe shined. They looked like businessmen. One of the men in a brown suit, who had taken the offering, came to me with a big smile and *Bible* under his arm, asked if I remembered him. I said I did not. He said, "I've been here for the last three months and will be going home to my family.   My name is Tom.   I'm the one you prayed with on Madison Avenue."

Probationary Lieutenant

In the spring of 1953 I was appointed as a probationary Lieutenant to four weeks at the School for Officer Training as a helper at the Brengle Memorial Institute. From the school I was sent to the Northern Divisional camp outside of Minneapolis for the remainder of the summer as the program director. My official appointment was as the assistant officer of the Virginia Minnesota Corps. At the end of camp my appointment was changed to the assistant officer of the St. Paul Citadel Corps where I arrived after two weeks' vacation. I was given a room at a nearby Y.M.C.A. where I spent the next year.

A picture of me in 1953 as a probationary Lieutenant

George Cleveland

George Cleveland, the son of the school principal from Tuttle, North Dakota, had come to Jamestown High School in his junior year. He was a tall, gangly, awkward guy with a dark crew cut. When he tried out for the basketball team, he had a difficult time handling the ball and was one of the first cut from the squad. Everyone laughed when he said, "I live and breathe basketball."

I took him on as a friend. As the year went on I realized that he was in a class by himself. He was staying with his uncle who lived on the hill west of my brother Leonard's house. He and I went to all the basketball games in town. When I gave my testimony during the street meetings, he stood around the corner and listened. When my mother went to the hospital, he was always someone I could talk to. George was liked by everyone in our school graduating as the valedictorian of our class.

As I was getting ready for my two weeks' vacation after camp, I got a call from Leonard that George had died and the family wanted me to come to the funeral in Tuttle. I rode with a carload of friends from high school. I wore my uniform and was invited to the house by the family who told me that I was George's best friend. They said that George had gone out to Washington State to find me the summer we graduated. He had gone to college and while attending an outing that summer he had drowned.

While going down the hallway in the St. Paul Y.M.C.A. several months later, I ran across the young pastor who had done the funeral. He told me the rest of the story. George had gotten "saved" and was at a church picnic and slipped on a raft and fell into deep water. By the time they got to him he had drowned. The pastor thought that he was attending a *Bible* college at the time.

St. Paul Saints

I spent a year in Saint Paul working with Captain and Mrs. Aden Read and their three children. The corps had a good band and averaged around one hundred in Sunday school. There were about fifty teenagers and young adults that became my friends. Following are three stories from that corps.

Mrs. Jack Fisher

She had been kicked in the face by a horse. The doctors had done their best for that day, but most of her lower jaw was missing. Every Sunday she was dressed in a full Salvation Army uniform including the bonnet. She had been commissioned as the Young People's Sergeant Major, which meant she led most of the youth activities. She had a high raspy voice and carried a handkerchief in one hand to cover the drool when she spoke.

Her husband Jack, who had been gassed in World War I, brought her to the corps every week. She sold the Salvation Army *War Cry* at the capitol building for over thirty years where weekly she witnessed to every governor and his staff who knew her by her first name.

She told of meeting Samuel Logan Brengle at the corps in Grand Forks, North Dakota, when she was nineteen. At the time she was in college to become a nurse. Her face had been deformed several years before. While praying with her at the altar, he gave her these words that she quoted often: *"From all the care of what men think or say, Cleansing for me. From ever fearing to speak, sing, or pray, Cleansing for me. Lord, in Thy love and Thy power make me strong, That all may know that to thee I belong. When I am tempted let this be my song. Cleansing for me."*

Gus Johnson

Gus and his wife were in full uniform every Sunday. He would testify of his days as a drunk. After his conversion he had started a jail ministry. He told of his six children, the first three of whom had gone bad and several had spent time in jail. After he became a Christian his last three children were active workers in the corps. He always believed that all his children would get right with God.

He and his wife had me to their house for dinner almost every week.

The Zimmermans

The Zimmermans came in late to the corps meetings walking in a line, father, mother, beautiful daughter and son. They would sit toward the front, the mother and father in full uniform. They looked a little like Ma and Pa Kettle. Their son Doug was smart but always looked a little unkempt. The daughter was a blonde with a perfect complexion and looked like the daughter of the Munsters.

The father gave the following testimony almost every week. When he was nineteen he had lived on a farm in Minnesota with his parents and had given up going to church. One evening he had gone into town to drink at a tavern with some friends. The hour grew late so he had to walk home in the dark taking a shortcut through a field and an old abandoned farmyard. As he made his way in the moonlight, he could see the outline of empty buildings. A light dusting of snow covered the path. He had too much to drink and didn't know exactly where he was.

As he walked he felt boards under his feet give way and he fell into a hole. He realized that he had dropped into the farmer's well. In that part of the country some wells were sixty to seventy feet deep. As he hung there he wondered if they had filled in the well when they left the farm. Every time he moved, the boards creaked. When he tried to free himself, the boards gave way a little more.

He looked up at the stars and promised God if He would spare him he would give up drink and serve him all the days of his life. He called out for help, but no one came. When he could hold on no longer, he let go and dropped a few feet onto the rocks below. He thanked God that he had planned for him years before when the farmer had filled in the well. He said he had never gone back on God from that day on.

Betty Chapin

An old friend Envoy Donald Lovejoy asked me to go along with him to Chicago, so he could visit his wife who was in the Training College. My old girlfriend had told me she was getting married to someone else so I was free and looking. Goldie was a cadet from Minneapolis whom I had some interest in. When we got to the school, I went in to visit with the cook, who had been my friend from the year before, who told me that Goldie had gone with her mother and would not be back until later.

The cook then began to introduce me to those in the kitchen as her best helpers from the last session. After an introduction to four of five cadets a girl cadet came out of the pantry, and the cook said, "This is Cadet Betty Chapin." Then I remembered Laura's word, "The perfect girl for you!" I said, "Oh, you are Betty Chapin; how interesting, nice to meet you." I never did get to talk to Goldie.

Off to the Clinic

In the summer of 1954 I was "farewelled" to Rochester, Minnesota, as the assistant officer. The corps had a big band and Sunday school. I stayed in one of the rooms in the Army's hotel unit on the second floor of the corps building making my meals in the corps's kitchen in the basement. Many people came to the Mayo Clinic and stayed in one of our six rooms.

One of the Sons

One day while I was tending the office, a very clean well dressed cowboy came in looking for help. He was out of money and needed food and a place to stay while he went to the clinic. He said he had been told by his doctor that he had only weeks to live.

I didn't recognize his name but I knew his face. When I asked him who he was, he said he was one of the Sons of the Pioneers.

We helped him with a room and meals for several weeks and he went on his way.

The Rings

I sold about seventy *War Crys* every week going from store to store. I had fallen in love with Lieutenant Betty Chapin and needed rings to get things moving along. I was going to Kenosha, Wisconsin, to see her. As I passed by a jewelry store I saw the 25 percent sign on wedding rings. I went inside to sell my magazine as usual and asked to see some rings. He knew my name and said he could make me a deal. I told him which rings I wanted, gave him the $95 I had saved from my salary of $19.50 a week, took the rings and left the next Monday to see Betty.

On Monday afternoon we were parked out by the lake when I took out my billfold to check my money. The ring fell out and she picked it up and asked what the ring was for. I said, "For you if you want it." She did, and has been wearing it for over fifty years.

When I got back to Rochester and my *War Cry* route, I went to the jewelry store to tell my friend I had given her the ring. He said he had made a big mistake and his father wanted the rings back because they had already been discounted by 40 percent and were valued at $175. I told him the rings were gone and I had no more money. He said he would need to consider it a donation to the Army.

Sunday School is Over

Every Sunday the Sunday school leader at the closing sang, "Sunday school is over and we a-going home, good by, good by." Fifty to sixty people got up and went out the front door. There might be the band and twenty to thirty people remaining in the audience. When the captain and his family went on vacation, I changed the words of the song to, "Sunday school is over and we are staying here, sit down, sit down." Most of them sat down. When I explained that we would sing one song and have a short message, they all stayed. When the captain came home, he asked me how I got them to stay. In several weeks they stopped singing anything about Sunday school being over with most people staying for the entire morning.

December, 1954, to Red Wing, Minnesota

The Divisional Commander called and told me they needed me in Red Wing, Minnesota, as the new officer in charge. That meant that I was the first of nine single male officers from my session to go in charge. The captain, who was being appointed to Chicago, said I should not make any of the people now attending the corps soldiers.

When I came to Red Wing, the corps building and officer quarters were in a storefront building downtown across from the Farmers Store. When I entered the building for the first time, I walked to the back room where the rummage was kept.

The clothing on an old couch at the back of the room began to move. A head popped out and said, "Who are you?" I said I was the new corps officer. I asked who he was and what he was doing in this locked-up building. He said his name was Donald Jay and the back door had been left unlocked. He often slept here on cold nights before going home to the farm. His face looked like a pizza with many pox marks. He said he would see me on Sunday and exited by the back door.

Betty Chapin.

December 6, 1955, Lieutenants Betty and Lester were married in the Fond du Lac Corps before family and friends.

Our wedding picture

Stephen Keith Anderson

Stephen was born on April 8, 1957, a year and a half later at what is now known as Fairview Red Wing Hospital (then it was St. John's Hospital). That year we purchased our first "OB" pug dog. We had gone to Minneapolis to Mrs. Daily's toy dog farm to buy a pug dog.

On the way home we stopped at the "Home and Hospital" to see a friend on the staff who were having the "O.K.'s" Christmas party for officers' kids. They said it was more of an "OB's" party-- Officers' Brats. We called our new pug our officer's brat. He slept under Stephens's bed in the front room and often protected him from unwanted visitors.

Mason

Mason was proud to be a full-blooded Sioux from the Prairie Island reservation about five miles north of town along the Mississippi River. He, his wife and two young daughters attended the corps most Sundays. Mason was short and usually dressed in a blue suit with a white shirt and a red bow tie. His hair was well groomed, but when he smiled you could see that he was missing one front tooth.

He liked to give his testimony at the street meetings down by the bars where he and his wife had been the town drunks. He had been thrown in jail for fighting. The corps officers, Major Mage Hojem and Captain Tulia Miller, had come to do their weekly jail meetings. After several visits Mason turned his life over to God and never returned to his old ways. When I arrived five years later, he was working as a contractor carrying his *Bible* and often holding meetings for the Sioux families in his home. He and his family were a light in a very dark place, and many Sioux looked up to him as their chief. He wanted to be sure that his girls married Sioux boys.

We had a Wednesday night prayer meeting that he and his family attended. One week I told him visitors from divisional headquarters were coming to check our corps out. He said he would bring some of his friends. After the meeting had started, the folks from the reservation arrived in groups until the hall was filled. Our visitors who had come the year before were impressed. After the meeting I told Mason he had done good and he gave his missing tooth smile.

Years later I heard that he and his family had moved to the Twin Cities where he became a building contractor. He had never wanted to live on the reservation or take the government's money. I was told he had started his own church.

Willie

Willie was a Sioux who attended the corps with Mason Walker before I arrived. He was six-foot-six and had been an all-state end in football with honors who had joined the Air Force and completed two years of service. He had a problem with his younger sixteen-year-old brother and two minor sisters. He said they needed to get right with God and brought them to the corps on Sunday morning. They came forward and asked God to forgive them and give them a chance to start over. They began to attend the corps; and when we discovered they could sing as a quartet, they often sang in the chapel and on the street.

A church in Minneapolis, "Souls Harbor," heard about their singing and invited them to come Sundays and sing on television to the whole state of Minnesota. When they asked me about what they should do, I told them that if God wanted them there it was all right with me. They began to attend there every week with the church giving them food and gas money. After several months had passed, Willie came to tell me his brother and sisters had all backslid and were back to their old ways. He was finished and was returning to the Air Force. We never saw them again while we were stationed there.

Thirty-five years later when we were stationed in Kansas City, we were taking part in a big event in the downtown area. A police officer came and asked if there was a Lieutenant Anderson here. The head of security wanted to talk to me. When I came up to the head of crowd control, he turned around and there was Willie. He told me how he had attended the Army in Kansas City when he first moved here and played trombone in the band. When the new officer came, he and his wife did not feel welcome and moved with their family to a *Bible* Church. He assured me he was still serving God.

When I asked him how his family back in Red Wing was doing, he said his sisters were married and his brother had been elected chief of the tribe, and was in charge of the tribe and their very large casino. They have a village with many new homes and a school with a field for sports. When asked what he thought about everything, he said he never planned to go back to the reservation and did not want any of their money. Years later I saw a special television program that talked about the wealth of each of the 452 members of the Prairie Island Sioux Reservation. Willie was the winner.

Off To Winona

Divisional Headquarters (DHQ) told us we were getting a great appointment when they sent us off down the river to the lovely city of Winona, Minnesota. During our first month we announced to our Sunday morning congregation of about sixty people that we were having a street meeting before the evening service. They were all invited to attend. When it came time for the street service, about fifty of them showed up.

Mark Wayne Anderson

"It will be a boy. If it isn't a boy, it will be a girl." was grandmother Chapin's prediction. She was right again. It was a red-headed boy who moved in with us at 413 Vine Street. He was born at Winona General Hospital on December 4, 1958.

Two Boys in the Open Air

We had moved into the upstairs apartment above the corps building to save heat and rent money. The office was behind the chapel where the boys played safely away from Main Street. We called them but they were gone. We heard singing in front of our building. We found them: Mark, the two-year-old, with a ukulele and Stephen, the four-year-old, with a concertina singing "The B.I.B.L.E." at the top of their voices. People passing by smiled their approval; we clapped and told them how good they were doing.

Christmas Baskets

We cleared out the chairs from the chapel and lined the food baskets up row upon row. The Boy Scouts brought in over a thousand bags of canned goods from their residential food drive during the month of December. We sent out letters with the hour and day when the families were to come in for their food and toys. For three days our building was filled with people. It was a wonderful time of the year. On the last day we had heavy snows so some families came in late. We helped all the families who needed help even if they had not signed up. Finally our building was empty. We had given out all the food that came in.

It was Christmas Eve and several Advisory Board members had come by to drop off super food baskets for the officer's family. They told us it was a family tradition. I put the first one in the back office and told Betty where it was. It had food and a large ham with candy and toys for the boys. The second one came in as we were locking up. I thanked the donor and took it up the twenty-five steps to our apartment.

I went to the post office and when I returned I was met at the door by a man and his five children. Their car had broken down and they had just gotten a ride from a friend. I went to the back office and gave them the super basket. They thanked me and the father cried as he told me that this basket and toys were all they would have for Christmas. When I locked the front door, it was almost 7 p.m. and I had not had a thing to eat since noon.

When I reached the top of the stairs, I was greeted with a request to go down to the office and get the basket and toys. A needy family had come while I was away. As they had not been able to get here on time, my wife had given them the basket from our apartment. At first we all laughed when I told them how I had given away the basket from the office. Then we realized that we had little or nothing to eat. We had gifts for the boys but not as good as the ones in the basket.

We made do with a can of soup and bread with peanut butter. We would all go out and eat tomorrow at a nice restaurant. On Christmas Day we opened what presents we had and went to eat around noon. As we drove through the snow, we noticed that all the stores and restaurants were closed. No food in our apartment and no place to eat. There were no fast food restaurants then like there are today.

We drove out to the edge of town and saw that a little hot dog stand had its lights on. We drove up to find Nick the Greek just about to close his door. The best he had was a plate of spaghetti for each of us. The four of us sat at a table by the front window and ate our spaghetti Christmas dinner while the snow was covering the world outside. As time has passed I realize that this was one of the most meaningful Christmas dinners we had ever shared together.

A Better Standard of Living?

The lady from the city welfare office called and said I needed to come in for some instructions. The director, who had done her job for many years, informed me about the residency laws. When someone came in for help who was not from the county and had no visible means of support, we were to only give them help for one day. She asked us to send them to her for a bus ticket home. Her suggestion sounded sensible to me.

After several years she called and said there were to be some changes. They were closing her city office where she worked alone and opening a county office where there would be eight workers. They would be calling me later with instructions for any changes they wanted me to make. A year later they called and said they were closing the county offices and the new state welfare department would be taking care of things. They had a new office and over thirty employees. There were new federal laws that abolished the old residency laws. Now they would be helping everyone who came to them regardless of their residence.

I discovered that a family of four, who received $95 a month from Alabama in welfare, could come to Minnesota and get $285 a month. Before this change any one could come from Alabama to work in Minnesota if they could take care of their expenses. The flood gates were opened. Someone said that they understood that their family would vote in the next election for the party that made this move possible. All over America the northern states were invaded by those seeking a better standard of living. The result of the abolishing of the residency laws has been catastrophic to America. Is it possible that abolishing or not enforcing our border laws will cause even greater problems?

CHAPTER TEN

WHY NOT MINOT?

I had visited Minot, North Dakota, while playing for the Jamestown High School football team in 1951. There were many fine soldiers during that time. Some years later while stationed in Winona, Minnesota, I did special meetings there as a part of an officers' evangelistic team. Someone from headquarters mentioned that they were having a problem finding someone to follow the officer who had been there for eleven years. We were ready to move and I said we would go.

Christine Lynn Anderson

Christine was born in Minot at the St. Joseph Trinity Hospital on April 27 in 1964, which was our best blessing from there.

TV Christmas Kettle

We needed help raising money at Christmas time. There were twenty days in December that year of ten below zero or greater and winds of forty miles an hour. I went to the television station with the idea of an on-the-air kettle for children, which the manager agreed was a good idea. Would five minutes between the noon news and the county western show be good enough? They told me how to prepare the names and numbers for presentation. I did eighteen live shows bringing in money from four states and Canada. People whom I did not know greeted me on the street. Not only did children send in money but adults and companies helped us reach our goal.

Two Star General

We were stationed in Minot as corps officers for four years. About five airmen and their families from the Air Force base five miles north of the city attended the corps with many taking part in the band and Sunday school. One Sunday a new senior airman attended the Holiness Meeting. Most of the airmen stood when he entered the chapel. We discovered that he was a Salvationist from Pennsylvania who was the top noncom officer in charge of the base air police with many of our men under his command.

From time to time we would visit the families that lived on the base. I purchased a new Air Force raincoat with a hat cover that had come in our Family Service Store. It fit me and looked great with the uniform. I wore it for several weeks and thought it would look more like a Salvation Army coat if I put my captain's stars on the applets. No one made any comments.

One day while it was raining I drove my dark blue station wagon out to the base to visit our master sergeant recovering from an operation. I had on my new raincoat and hat cover. When I got to the gate, I told them that I was here to visit the master sergeant.

The guard looked in the rolled down window, snapped to attention and with a snappy salute waved me through. The other guards came out in the rain and gave me the same snappy salute.

When I arrived at the sergeant's quarters, I was greeted by his wife with a big smile. She said the gate had called and said there was a two-star general coming to visit us, where upon she helped me remove the stars from my applets. You might say it takes more than stars to make a general.

Corps Cadets in the Snow

We had twenty corps cadets between the ages of fourteen and eighteen who came early on Wednesday evening for lunch and stayed for classes and recreation. Once a month we would go on an outing. Since most of the cadets were from hardy Norwegian stock, we had planned a toboggan outing. The temperature had dropped below zero with 40-mile-an-hour winds, but the cadets would not take no for an answer.

Mrs. Anderson went to our quarters to make hot chocolate and chili. Eighteen of us loaded up the toboggans and went out to a hill on the edge of town. We climbed the hill and made our first run. All went well. We decided to make one more run and then go back to our warm house. We bounced down the hill to where our cars were parked, loaded the two wagons and got ready to go.

I had learned to take a count on teen outings. One Corps Cadet was missing. We called out in the cold freezing wind but there was no answer. Donna who had been riding on the back of the last toboggan was missing. The snow was deep. We had passed through a patch of sagebrush. If we didn't find her, she would freeze in a few minutes. The men and boys backtracked up the hill and found her unconscious under the snow in the brush where she had been bumped off. She woke up quickly when we shook her.

By the time we got back to our house, we were warm, happy and singing. When we called the hospital, they told us that if she had survived for this long she should be all right, to just keep her warm and put her feet in hot water. She survived.

Years later her beautiful blond Norwegian daughter was commissioned as a lieutenant from the Chicago Training College. If we hadn't taken a count when we left the building and the hillside, Donna would have frozen and her daughter would have never been. God works in mysterious ways his wonders to perform.

Gus, Gus, Gus

The Minot Corps sat on a hill west of downtown. Our bright red shield on blue sign could be seen from miles away. Most people had little difficulty in finding the corps building. The lady in the office called me and said that there was someone from the hospital here to see me. When I went to the top of the stairs, there on the lower landing stood Gus, the captain of my high school football team from fifteen years before, dressed in his white uniform and looking tired.

When he came to the top of the stairs, he asked if I remembered him. He had been "Never quit Gus," the plunging back who played even with a dislocated shoulder. The team looked to him for leadership. I remembered that several times he was standing around the corner by the Blackstone Hotel while I gave my testimony in the Jamestown Salvation Army street meeting.

He told a sad story about a drinking problem that had caused him to lose his family and was about to get him fired from his job at the hospital. He wanted me to help him, but what could I say? If he would have attended a meeting, I could have preached to him. I wasn't ready to meet his request. I shared with him some scripture verses and had a prayer. He seemed better when he left.

I told my wife that I had failed to give him much help. I set out to discover a way to share the message of salvation that he needed. For the next twenty years I learned how to share my faith and taught others how to do the same, always keeping in mind my failure with Gus.

At our thirty-fifth high school class reunion we were gathering at the American Legion hall. It was a day of fellowship and renewal ending with a dinner and a dance. I asked some of the fellows from the football team if they had heard from Gus. They said that he was in town, but he was only coming to the Sunday picnic in the park. He wouldn't come where drinks were being served. They said that he had stopped drinking many years ago. God works in mysterious ways his wonders to perform. It was possible that the day that we met together changed both of our lives.

The House by the River

An elderly couple visited our Salvation Army store every week. Winter or summer she wore the same elegant fur coat. He drove a black 1926 Studebaker roadster while she sat in the back seat and waved to the gawkers on the street. They came to the store to carry out the old shoes, papers and boxes of junk the clerk was throwing away telling us they were burning them in their cook stove.

They gave us their address so we decided we would visit them and invite them to our services. They lived in a big green three-story house down by the river not far from the train station. It had eleven bedrooms and at one time had been a boarding house where the famous actor Boris Karloff had spent some time in 1912.

When we drove in the yard it looked like a spook house from a "B" horror movie that Karloff might have starred in. (He had also lived in Minot, North Dakota, for a year performing in an opera house above a hardware store. For health reasons, he did not fight in World War I.)   The trees and lilac bushes had overgrown the wrought iron fence that squared their city block.

When we parked our car behind the ancient Studebaker, we noticed that the only light on was in the back kitchen area. We rapped on the front door and they waved us around to the back. When we got there, we saw movable wooden steps that were pushed up to a large kitchen window they pushed on which opened on hinges into the kitchen. They said that their house was so filled with boxes that they were living in this room and sleeping in a side room. We could see that every hallway was packed with boxes of shoes, papers, fruit jars, clothes and magazines. They said they hadn't been in the upstairs in years.

We read our *Bible* and prayed with them and after a half hour exited by the kitchen window. As we drove away we said that we had seen it all. Several weeks passed and she called crying that the fire department was refusing to put out the fire. She wanted us to come and help. When we got there, the firemen told us that they had tried to put the fire out but had decided that they were going to let it burn itself out. It burned and smoldered for five days. They said the rats had been running to the river every day.

A week later when we located them by phone to ask if we could help, she replied that they were doing just fine. They had purchased another big house that they had been living in for the past year. They had run out of room a long time ago. They had met us at their old house so we would be able to see how grand it was.

The Black Hills

A crowd of teenage corps cadets came to the airport in Minot to see the five of us off on Frontier Air Lines to our new appointment at Rapid City, South Dakota. Our Sunday school had gone from an average of seventeen to ninety plus for the past year. We had just completed our Children's Fair *Bible* School. We felt good about the work that had been done. When we arrived at the airport in Rapid City, we were greeted by about twenty teens and young adults. They welcomed us and helped with our baggage.

The corps had a band of twenty-five members. The Sunday school averaged around sixty each Sunday. Following are three stories of interest.

Cornet Player from God

The band, made up of eight college students, six or seven young adults and members from the air base, played Sunday morning and evening. When our solo cornet player left for college creating a problem, we decided to pray for a replacement. The next Sunday an airman, Gibe, arrived carrying a cornet case and asked if he could play with the band, but he ended up in the back row with the second cornets. We prayed more specifically for a great solo cornet player.

Several weeks later another airman arrived and asked if we had a band. He was a premier solo cornet player from the Southern Territory who had won contests. George picked up a cornet and played brilliantly. The band never sounded so good.

One cold winter Wednesday night he came to band practice and nearly fell off his chair. He had a little drinking problem. We had a meeting and decided we could not depend on George. A teenaged lead second cornet player said she would like to try playing the solo part, and in a few minutes we realized we had our soloist with us all the time. She got better with age.

Francis Was a Man

Francis was the father of five teenaged children and the husband of a Home League lady who taught Sunday school and worked at the Salvation Army store. He had a Catholic background, worked at a lumber company, smoked and was known to use swear words on most occasions. Bald and slightly built he never attended the corps for the first years we were in Rapid City although his family was very active.

One Thursday evening his wife was attending a corps growth training meeting. We were closing and had divided into teams to share the "Four Spiritual Laws" with each other. As I was sitting alone when he came to pick up his wife, he sat down by me and asked what we were doing. I explained that they were sharing a booklet and I had no partner to share it with. When I asked if he would like to help me, he said OK, and I proceeded to share the "Laws" with him. He prayed the prayer and the meeting ended. We had united prayer and all went home.

The oldest daughter called several days later and asked what I had done to their father. He was a changed man. He attended the meetings regularly and was truly changed, soft spoken and a good friend.

Twenty years later we attended the corps while on vacation in the Black Hills and were pleased to see Francis in full Army uniform giving the announcements and praying for the offering. Ten years later when he was 80, while visiting I prayed with him at the altar. He told me he was ill and the doctor had informed him that he had only a little while left. He said he was ready. He was a man of God.

Chief of the Ogallala Sioux

Martin was a full-blooded Sioux whose grandmother told him of her part in the battle of the Little Bighorn. She said that the women of the Sioux went out with butcher knives and cut up the soldiers. They did not cut up Custer. Martin had married a white schoolteacher and been one of the nation's top bronco riders. When his wife died he sold his ranch, went on a drinking binge and lost all his money in Las Vegas. He was wise enough to keep his water rights. The Sioux men stepped aside when he walked down the street. At the end of the month the ranchers lined up to pay for their water.

He wore Tony Lama boots, the best western hat and stylish clothes. When he went on a drunk, he would hide until he was sober. He would make dates with much younger women and bring them to his room after dark. He worked as our janitor when he was sober and lived in a white house north of the corps building.

One afternoon I drove him out to our Thunderhead Falls Camp in the Black Hills. I wanted him to work on our council ring before we started summer camp. It was late in the afternoon and I had to get back to the corps so I suggested that he stay and work until dark and then spend the night in our lodge. He said, "Don't leave me here because we know that Spooks come out at night. No Indians will stay in the hills after sundown."

Martin was going to get right with God at a later date. When he retired he received a monthly check. He got his own place and began drinking with his friends. One day while we were out of the city, he ran out of money and began drinking rubbing alcohol ending up in the hospital in a coma. A nurse, who attended the corps, said his daughter called a priest, but all that Martin would say was "Major, Major, Major." The family didn't know what he was trying to say. Martin was ready to get right with God. I shall never forget what I couldn't do for Martin.

The Star of Lights

Up the block from the corps building was the thirteen-story Tri-State Milling Company building. The owners had placed a large star at the very top with thirty-five light bulbs that could be seen from fifteen miles away during the Christmas season. I asked them if they would let us make it our "Star of Lights." They agreed and we planned to change the lights from red to white for each thousand dollars we accumulated for Christmas.

We reported each day to the media how many lights were lit. The star changed from red to white as we reached our goal by Christmas Eve. We did this for the four years we were there. Every year we had eighteen days to give the live television Christmas kettle message. The station reached into five states so we were greeted by many people we did not know.

Gold in Them There Hills

Albert Eckland had discovered Thunderhead Falls while exploring the Black Hills. Miners in the late 1800s had tried to divert Rapid Creek at "The Big Bend" by cutting through the mountain. They cut from both directions to divert the water and missed their mark creating what today is known as "Thunderhead Falls." The Big Bend Gold Mine was worked as a placer mine by over one hundred men for over fifteen years. When wages went to two dollars a day and gold sold for two dollars an ounce, the mine was closed.

Eckland gave the seventeen acres to the Salvation Army while we were the corps officers in 1970. He continued placer mining into his eighties making between three hundred and four hundred dollars a month by panning gold. He showed some of us how he did it telling us the mine was still full of gold. He ended up giving his home and land to the Army. The camp is still used by the Army and other churches.

CHAPTER ELEVEN

OFF TO THE TWIN CITIES

After four long action-filled years we were moved to Minneapolis as the Citadel Corps officers. We were moving back to the Northern Division where I had grown up. The corps was in the Divisional Headquarters building and was made up of officers and old Army families. The band played Sunday morning and evening. The quarters were in St. Louis Park and were very small. Here are several stories I remember.

The Man from Hollywood

Dick had worked in Hollywood in his younger days, but noted that his name never appeared on any of the credits. He was our fundraiser, *War Cry* seller, and Corps Sergeant Major. He said he sold the *War Cry* by the page. When he led a song or asked for the offering, he sounded like a carnival barker. He loved to collect HO trains and bought a new train almost every week.

He raised over three hundred dollars every week. His biggest success was in "gifts-of-kind." One of the companies that donated items was Music Land: five hundred guitars and other stringed instruments that could be repaired and sold, one truck-load of phonograph records in fifty cases with hundreds in each case and radios and other electronics by the case, Wedgwood seconds by the case, and Tortino's pizzas by the case. He was a big help and made it possible to carry on a good corps program.

God's Bible Man

Major David Carlson was a stocky baldheaded Swede who spoke broken English and spent most of his career as an open-air preacher and Service Extension fundraiser in northern Minnesota. He never married and would get on the bus on Monday morning in Minneapolis and travel from city to city with his *Bible*, briefcase and guitar. When he got off the bus, he would conduct a one-man street meeting. When everyone knew that he had arrived, he would start down the street preaching and collecting money, some of which he would leave with the local Army committee. He was Mr. Salvation Army to most of northern Minnesota for years.

When he turned sixty-five they told him he could quit now and take a rest. He wandered the streets of downtown Minneapolis and finally retreated to his hotel room. When they went to visit him, he said he needed something to do, and they sent him back out on the road for another ten years. Every year at officers' councils he would stand and wave his *Bible* and tell all the officers we needed to get out and go to work.

When our family arrived in Minneapolis, he was in his eighties and needed to go to a rest home. We would pick him up for early morning open-air meetings before the Sunday morning meeting. One morning while he was giving his testimony, someone threw an egg from an open apartment window that spattered on his uniform. He wore the spatter as a medal for the rest of the day. He was faithful to the end.

Casey and Roundhouse Rodney

In their prime the Casey Jones programs, especially his noontime Lunch with Casey, were the most popular children's shows, not only in the Twin Cities but throughout Minnesota and surrounding states where WTCN was available over cable systems. I went by the station in the Lake of the Isles area near the corps building and spoke to the program manager about Salvation Army television Christmas kettle announcements. He said he would get back to me. When I stopped by to see what they had decided to do, they introduced me to Casey and Roundhouse. They liked the idea and wanted me to start the day after Thanksgiving.

I checked with DHQ and they said, "Ya, sure, what did you say you were going to do? Who are Casey and Roundhouse?" I did eighteen days for each of the next two Decembers. Wherever I went the children and mothers smiled and greeted me as "Major Anderson." The first time it happened I asked Mrs. Anderson who those people were. She reminded me about the television show.

Casey and Roundhouse became our friends. Roundhouse, who was a preacher, came on Sunday evening and did a gospel message in his own unique way. He stood on his hands and threw rubber fruit off the wall to get his point across. The total Salvation Army Christmas effort for the Twin Cities went up by fifteen percent which they attributed to their PR department. I told the Army story every day and asked the adults to send their contributions to help us reach our goal as I had in Minot and Rapid City.

City Wide Evangelism

The seven corps of Minneapolis and St Paul united for five nights of evangelism visitation training. We started with an all night of prayer at the Temple Corps where Major and Mrs. Chet Sundman were the corps officers. All seven corps took part with the meetings starting at 9:00 p.m. and ending with a breakfast after the 6:00 a.m. meeting.

There were over 100 persons present for every meeting. A delegation from every corps attended the five nights of two-hour training sessions. All corps were to conduct five nights of visitation evangelism. The Minneapolis Citadel had thirteen men and three women who visited over two hundred homes with twenty-five seekers.

At our last report meeting one elderly man, who had taken part in all five nights, told us that he had been the black sheep of his family of eight children. He wondered if his mother and father in heaven would know that after fifty years of sin and drunkenness that he had gotten saved and tonight he had led an old man to Christ. We told him that even the angles in heaven were rejoicing so his mother and father would surely know.

Forever Fifty Club.

We had about twenty-five seniors who were attending an Arts and Craft Club that we were holding in the Citadel Basement Hall. I was giving drawing and painting lessons every week and other members were teaching and displaying the crafts. We were going on outings and having lunch together.

A Baptist Church from south Minneapolis brought in a Christmas offering from their Forever Fifty *Bible* class. I liked the name and asked if they would let me use it for our senior club. They said I was welcome to the name. We printed a large yellow pin with red letters that said "Forever Fifty." The Divisional Commander used the name for all the senior clubs in the Northern Division. That name is still in use thirty years later.

The Lake of the Isles

Many of the new people who joined the corps were from this rich area. One older man named Bob owned a white six-story apartment house. His wife had recently died and he needed friends. He would relate the week's events as he left the morning holiness meeting. He lived in the top apartment and told us that he had fallen asleep in his easy chair and had heard someone at his front door. Usually he was at work at this time and as he went to open the door he heard voices. He went over and stood behind a cabinet full of collectables in the semidarkness.

Three men in white jumpsuits snapped the lock and entered with bags and boxes. He stood there shaking as the men opened all his cabinets and removed his collectables, praying that they would not see him and would leave without hurting him. After they were gone, he called the police who informed him that they had broken into other homes and hurt some of the residents. He asked me if I thought God was watching over him. I told him for sure God had provided for him.

Other people from the area who attended the corps were the property manager for Billy Graham's Northwestern College, a vice president from Swift, and a publisher of the Minnesota Twins game programs.

CHAPTER TWELVE

CHICAGO BELMONT

The word from headquarters was that our time was finished in Minneapolis and we were needed in Chicago. We packed our camper and moved to the big city where we spent four years as the corps officers of a growing sophisticated soldiery. Some wonderful things happened as related in the following stories.

The Streets of Chicago

The corps building was located on Belmont Avenue which ran east and west, and near the cross street of Sheffield running north and south. The intersection divided the neighborhood into four ethnic groups. Northeast was an area where three hundred Appalachians families had moved to work at a steel factory in North Chicago. In Southeast were somewhere between three hundred to four hundred Cuban and Puerto Rican families. To the Southwest were hundreds of Polish and German families who had lived there for years. The four blocks of Sheffield going south were filled with thirty gypsy families who wintered in the area. Northwest was made up of large and small businesses. Belmont Avenue traffic was always on the move.

The Army had the only playground in the area that was open to the public. Most of the time children were in our yard playing basketball, baseball, or field hockey. Headquarters called one cold winter evening and informed us that the police had called and said there was a riot down on our playground. During our four years as the officers we organized field hockey which involved about sixty boys. It was the night of the championship playoff. When the police realized it was a game and not a war, they wished us well and departed.

A Home with Room to Paint Pictures

Some changes had been made in the Chicago leadership. Lt. Colonel Andrew S. Miller had been appointed as the leader of the Army in the greater Chicago area. With him came many new ideas. The officers were allowed to purchase new quarters where they were needed. When we arrived our quarters were small and greatly in need of repair with holes in the walls and sideboards where we could look out through the open cracks. When the cold wind blew from the north, snow would come into the bedrooms.

We looked at nearly forty different homes with none of them meeting the Army's requirements. Most real estate agents misrepresented the property and we learned to detect the true age of a building by checking the date on the lid of the toilet stool water tank.

One day our realtor showed us the outside of a very nice Georgina style house in a better section of our district. She told us the owner was ill and would not let anyone inside to see the home. When she told us the price, I told her we would take it sight unseen. After she went to the door and told the wife we would buy the house, we were let in to meet her sick lawyer husband. They had not cleaned the house in years. A path had been worn in the rug from the chairs to the television. A full basement looked well suited for an art studio.

While walking down Belmont Avenue toward the bank, I noticed an office supply store with artist paint supplies in the window. Some were old and faded. There were boxes of oil paints, brushes and books on how to paint. Noticing my uniform they offered to sell me the lot at a greatly reduced price. I had not painted for many years.

I read the books and tried to paint in a way the books suggested every Tuesday night while Betty was at Home League. The painting of Samuel Logan Brengle that has hung in the Black Chair lounge of the Chicago school for Officer Training along with ten others was painted during that time.

After we moved in and fixed the house up, we were told by an officer from headquarters that we had one of the finest Army quarters in Chicago. Within weeks we were offered double what we had spent on it. Mayor Daley had passed a rule that all police and firemen that worked in Chicago, had to live within the city limits. God was with us.

The house was within four blocks of Skokie and was within walking distance of several Jewish synagogues and the largest Jewish high school in Chicago. We built a garage and had the backyard fenced in so we could go from the car to the house in safety.

Big Boys Basketball

Bob who. came to the corps was a part-time coach in the park leagues. He wanted to make up a team of friends to represent the Belmont Corps in the Salvation Army city league. We bought ten first class blue and white uniforms and fielded a team which came in second out of sixteen teams the first year. The players did not attend any of the corps meetings, so after several years we dropped the team.

I went out on the playground and asked several of the older boys who played every day, if they would like to put together a team to represent the Belmont Corps. They said they would attend the corps if they could bring their girlfriends. We agreed and six boys showed up the first night to play in the league during the next season.

The first week I went along as they played in a church gym across from the famous Cabrini-Green housing projects. The boys played well together and won by twenty points. The next week they added two more players and went to the South Side Settlement without me, where they played an all men's team. Some one called me and said the score was 125 to 36. I felt sorry for the boys until I found out that they had won the game. For the rest of the season they scored over 100 points in every game and kept the other teams below 50 points.

They were the talk of the town. I asked them to tell me why

they played so well. They said they were a team in the regular city league and played three or four nights a week.

They had all been stars in their high school teams with some having been the captain.

More than a Stick

We had an active program for the teens and young adults on the street of Chicago.   One of the tallest boys had the name of "Stick." His family ran a tavern three blocks north of the corps building and most nights you could find him on our playground shooting hoops. He joined our teams and was a star in basketball. He had been on the winning field hockey team and was to receive a trophy at our upcoming sports banquet.

The television news broke the story of his twenty-five-year-old brother's suicide. He had taken his revolver and shot himself in front of Stick, warning him that he had destroyed himself by using drugs. We went to visit the family and the father blamed God for this son's problems. We read the scriptures and prayed.   Two nights later we held the banquet which consisted of two sloppy Joes, a Coke and chips. All sixty boys showed up. Colonel Norman Marshall gave a message about being a winner. We concluded with the "Four Laws" presentation.

All the boys filled out a card with their names and whether or not they prayed the prayer. After the meeting and the boy had left, we checked the cards and discovered that Stick was one of the boys who had made a decision.   He began to attend some of the corps meetings. The Colonel was moved by the story and told it at THQ devotions the next day.

Junior Soldiers

It is important to decide what the most essential program is for the youth of the corps. The streets around the Chicago Belmont Corps were filled with children who needed some direction. We understood that we had to give them the best hours of the week, the best rooms in our building and our best youth leadership. We set a goal to have fifty active Junior Soldiers involved in this corps programs.

We decided to divide them into two groups; those from six to eleven were given red jackets and those from twelve and up were given blue Senior Soldier blue jackets. To exchange the jacket or to get a new one if they lost theirs, they were asked to pay fifty cents. We put together workbooks using the guard and sunbeam merit badges. We met every week, the younger red coats after school and the older blue coats at seven.

We limited our groups to twenty-five each with separate leadership. Every child was given an introduction session which explained the program and explained how to be saved and born again. The power and success of this program was the stress on the spiritual importance of being a Soldier. In a short while we had the fifty Junior Soldiers and eight qualified leaders.

We kept records for one year and were asked to make a presentation of the program to all the divisional leaders. Many of them wanted to start at once. We told them it would take some time to set up the material. We met with territorial leaders and they agreed to look into the matter. They sent us out as youth leaders with encouragement to use this program in that division. When the territorial commander changed, the program was put aside. We continued to use this program until we retired.

One Hundred Children March

Our Junior Soldiers would march when we had our yearly children's fair (*Bible* School). With flags flying and a small band playing they would march around the block attracting other children in the neighborhood. By the end of the five-day fair we would have well over one hundred children in the march. One of our rules was the daily, "Silent Good Deed" that required each child to do something helpful without being recognized or thanked for their effort.

The local grade school officials called and asked the office what we were doing to these children. They told us the children were cleaning up the playground and helping wherever they could without being asked. On the day of their meeting they all wore their red jackets so the school knew who they were. The school officials told us not to stop our program.

The One-A-Day Club

We conducted a "Way of L.I.F.E. Worship Seminar," and during week seven we shared material on "How to Introduce Others to Christ." We invited eighty people in the morning Holiness Meeting to join together to share their faith this next week.   Seventeen people remained after the Sunday evening meeting.

Basically it involved sharing the "Four Spiritual Laws" with the first person we were alone with for five minutes where the Holy Spirit opened up the way. We were to do this every day for one week. We banded together after some instructions and started on Sunday night after the meeting and reported the next Sunday. The following stories are related to this program.

Margo

While in Minneapolis I had been talked into getting a hairpiece that I had been wearing for two years when we arrived at the Belmont Corps. I had decided to get one from a professional hairdresser. A shop on Lincoln Avenue had a sign in the window that said wigs for men and women. When I went inside, the owner took me to a back room and brought out several hair pieces for me to try on.

I sat in the barber chair, and as time passed I realized that my five minutes were up and we started talking about spiritual things. I took out my copy of the "Laws" and began sharing them with her. She listened and asked some questions. When we finished she informed me that she had been a student at the Moody Bible Institute. She said she had stopped attending her church on North

Avenue some years ago because she had been attacked by street dogs when she got out of her car. She asked if it would be all right if she came to our meetings. I told her that we would be pleased to have her and her family come. She gave me the number of another hair shop and told me I would get a new hairpiece at her cost. I thanked her and left not knowing if she would attend.

When Sunday morning came, I had gone to stand by the front door to welcome the regular members when a new gold Cadillac pulled up by the front door. A finely dressed lady and two children got out and came up the stairs. It was Margo and two of her grandchildren.

In the coming years she and her husband became members of the corps. She owned three shops on Lincoln Avenue, two Ford City Camera shops, a home in the suburbs and a summer home in Fox Lake. She became Home League secretary and eventually Corps Sergeant Major. She bought the corps a new van, and became a great supporter of the corps. One corps officer said that she and her husband took his family to dinner every Sunday. She was honored as the North Chicago Church woman of the year. Her picture in full uniform was on the cover of their publication.

Barbara

Barbara had two children and was part of the neighborhood Polish community. Sometimes she came to our Home League and Holiness meetings. One Sunday while standing at the end of the meeting she responded to the challenge to start over with God's help. She was a changed person and joined the One-A-Day Club; took her seven booklets on Sunday evening and returned by noon on Monday morning asking for more. We told her that she was not to give them away but to share them. She said she had shared them.

Several days later while I was walking down the street passing by a typewriter shop, the owner came out and remarked that we had a terrible lady down at the Salvation Army named Barbara. He warned me not to believe anything she said about him.

I discovered that she had been a street prostitute for several years. Her ex-husband, who worked for a big Chicago newspaper, had divorced her and married a rich woman from the suburbs, and came by Barbara's house for free sex several times a week. She had locked the door on him and told him that she had gotten saved and was living a changed life. He called me and threatened my life for what I had done for her. She kept witnessing and brought many of her old friends to the corps. She and her children became members of the corps.

Mary

Mary worked at Cook County Hospital and as a floor supervisor had the keys and access to the drug cabinets. She attended our meetings with one of her neighbors but always appeared to be sick. She volunteered to help with *War Cry* sales after her work. During one of our Sunday morning meetings she prayed to receive Christ. She got saved.

The next Sunday she looked like a new person. She came by the office and asked what we needed in the way of office equipment. She bought a new typewriter for Mrs. Anderson's office. The next week she gave a check to cover the cost of twenty-five new *Bibles* for the chapel. The next week she purchased ten sets of *Bible* study tapes at twenty-five dollars each. When asked why she was giving so much money to the corps, she said that was what she had been spending for drugs. She told us that she had called her family and led both her mother and father to the Lord.

Several Sundays later she came forward to the altar with a stack of books and other paraphernalia. She said that she had been a practicing witch and had left the coven.

The other witches had loaded her storage space with stolen merchandise and then called the police. I was called to go to court with her as a character witness. She was cleared of all charges. After some time she came in and said she had to move back home to Kentucky to hide on her family's horse farm. The witches had threatened her life. One day she was gone leaving no forwarding address.

No One on the Other End of the Line

We were receiving phone calls at supper time. No one would reply when we asked who it was; we would only hear heavy breathing. I decided it was a good time to share my faith, so I asked the person to stay on the line and listen to the message of God's Love. They did not hang up the phone and listened for ten minutes until I shared the prayer and thanked them for calling.

Several days had passed when the phone rang again. Without an introduction, a small voice began to sing, "I've anchored my soul in the haven of rest and I'll sail the wide seas no more..." The person finished the entire song and hung up and never called again.

The Stained Glass Window

I was working late in our front office when the phone rang. The man on the other end of the line said that he had passed our building and from the bus had seen the window with the picture of Christ and the lost sheep. He lived in Evanston and had decided to end his life by jumping into Lake Michigan. He had lost his job and after years of drinking had been locked out of his home by his wife.

I told him that God could change his life and help him to become a new person. I explained God's plan of salvation and he prayed to receive Christ over the phone. We were able to get him into the Harbor Light program, and he returned home sober three months later.

Four Years Later

The band in full uniform was on duty every Sunday morning and evening; we had enrolled fifty Junior Soldiers and more than forty Senior Soldiers. Our uniformed workers were selling 1,500 *War Crys* every week on the North side of Chicago. The entire corps bills were paid. We had sent five cadets into training. God had blessed our days in Belmont.

Michigan - God's Country

We were called to go to Divisional Headquarters in Grand Rapids, Michigan, as youth leaders for the twenty-six corps. The records showed that there were one hundred eighty corps cadets, fifteen corps bands, many corps with over a hundred in Sunday school. We were delighted to work with the officers and soldiers of such a great Army. The Territorial leaders wanted us to try our Junior Soldiers program in ten of the corps. They planned to use it throughout their other two hundred fifty plus corps. I was also allowed to conduct Soul Winning Seminars in all the corps.

A Butterscotch House

Stephen stayed in Chicago for his first year of college at the Chicago School of Education. He attended the Belmont Corps and played in the Chicago Staff Band. Mark and Christine moved with us into the small quarters, on the east side of Grand Rapids, that had just room enough for a pug dog and the four of us. The house was nestled at the foot of a hill with a small pine forest, a good place to cross-country ski in the winter. The house was freshly painted in two tones of butterscotch. Not much space but a good place to come home to. We attended the Grand Rapids Temple Corps and played in the band when we were in the city.

We visited most of the corps as a family the first year; the second year Mark and Christine stayed home and attended the corps on their own. Every corps we visited on Sunday had a covered dish dinner. We did one corps in the morning and one in the evening. We learned how to let all the cooks know that we had tried their dish.

Our neighbors had decided to have an outdoor pig-roast with all the trimmings. We paid the twenty-five dollars for the four of us and waited for the big event. On the Friday before the big day they dug a pit and began roasting the pig over a bed of hot coals. They poured beer over the meat. For every can they poured on the roasting pig they drank one. As the sun came up there were three neighbors sleeping by a burnt pig. They tried to cut the meat but their wives called for help. My days as a boy in a butcher shop paid off. I cut the meat into pork chops and everyone had a great lunch.

Our family planted a pine tree in the backyard after Christmas. Ten years later we visited the house and saw the beautiful full grown tree covered with snow

The Job: Divisional Youth Secretary

Our main assignment was to work with the corps officers and their youth programs. We were to see that all rolls and records were in proper order and give advice and encouragement when needed. When we were visiting one of the northern corps, the Lieutenant told of her loneliness. She said she was going home to find a husband. I told her she should stay at her post and the Lord could provide her with a young man to send to officers' training. She asked if that could really happen; I assured her that it could.

Six months later after the review she told me that she had someone she wanted me to meet. She took me out to the Burger Chef restaurant and introduced me to the chef. This nice young man was getting ready to go to training. His father owned three restaurants, which one day could be his. They married and went on to spend many years as fine corps officers.

Corps Cadets in the Water

All cadets with their lessons up to date were invited to go on a canoe trip on the Apple River. Sixty Corps Cadets and leaders showed up for the fifteen-mile trip. Stops were planned for lunch and rest. Thirty canoes started out with leaders out in front and following behind to make sure all would arrive safely. At our first stop the last canoe did not show up. That was before cell phones so we were not able to contact them and went on without them.

Twenty-nine canoes went on down the swirling river and finished before dark. Our bus was waiting to take us back to our cars and home. The driver told us that our experienced follow-up team had swamped their canoe around the first bend and gone home. We had other outings which brought many new young people into the program.

Visitation Teams

We conducted training seminars in the use of "The Four Spiritual Laws" and the *How to be filled with the Holy Spirit* booklet in all twenty-six corps The corps officer at Grand Rapids Citadel wanted to do the door-to-door team visitation. We did five nights of training and conducted five nights of visitation. One of the soldiers, who came in his wheelchair, wanted to take part so we set him up with a telephone visitation program where he could share his faith over the phone.

After several days the Captain called and asked me to go with him to this man's house because his phone was off the hook. When we got inside we found that he had died with his telephone in his hand and his *Bible* open to the verses he was sharing. He had died doing what he thought God wanted him to do.

A Change in Administration

When there was a change in Territorial leaders, the new leaders did not show interest in our Junior Soldiers programs and replaced us as youth leaders. We were appointed as corps officers to Battle Creek, Michigan.

CHAPTER THIRTEEN

OFF TO BATTLE CREEK

After three years at Divisional Headquarters we were moved to Battle Creek, Michigan, as the corps officers. This corps had at one time been one of the larger corps in Michigan. We were told that many years earlier there had been a feud between the Corps Sergeant Major and the corps officer over whose son should marry a lovely young lady who attended the corps. The corps officer won and the C.S.M. left for another church with many of the top soldiers. That church was having the largest Sunday school attendance in the city when we arrived in Battle Creek.

The Salvation Army Sunday school was running around forty in attendance and Sunday evening service was attended by about fifteen people.

Events that Brought About Change in the Corps

We had been telling people in the division how to grow a corps for the last three years. We put into action the plan we had told others to use. We visited our soldiers, set and posted advanced goals for the next four years, shared our faith and started visitation training classes. We began our Junior Soldiers classes with trained leaders. We did thirteen weeks of the "The Way of Life Seminar" every year. In a short time our meetings were well attended and new people came every week.

Man Sent by God - J. Paul Woody

On the day we arrived we were told the custodian, who had been living in the corps building apartment, had passed away and we needed to find a replacement. He had been a chain smoker, the apartment smelled of smoke and needed to be cleaned and repainted. The building was a sad cold place that needed the touch of God. Saturday morning one of the corps cadets called and said we should come to the office at once.

There were two people in an old green station wagon that had come to the building and told him that, "God had sent them to help us!" When we arrived and talked to the couple from Taccoa, Georgia, we discovered that God had called them a month earlier to leave their home and come to Michigan because there was a work for them to do. They said, "This must be the place; we are ready to go to work."

They moved into the apartment as it was and began to clean it up. They looked a little like Ma and Pa Kettle and stayed for the four years we were there. They became soldiers and made the building a warm and friendly place, and helped in many ways. His favorite thing was the Sunday Night Supper Club that helped fill the building and the altar on Sunday evening.

In the winter when he was asked to pick up people for the meetings, he would get out of his car with his *Bible* and touch the four corners of his car asking God to protect him. Those who rode with him said they could understand why he prayed before he drove. Many nights when we came into the building unannounced, we would hear him praying in the chapel at the top of his voice for the people. They loved the common people and made the building a warm and friendly place. They had been sent by God.

Street Meetings Bring Hope to Lost Souls.

One Sunday evening in April a young man and his nephew were returning from a church gathering; when they got off the bus, they passed by our open-air meeting. The band was playing, "Down at the Cross" while the soldiers and officers were singing the words over a portable public address system. A small crowd gathered across the street so the two went unnoticed. We gave a message that declared the good news of the gospel. The young man seemed to hang on every word, as if he were hearing the story for the first time.

When the message and last song were over, the young man crossed the street to speak to me. He asked who we were and where we were going after this meeting. We told him that we were God's Army and that we would be having a meeting in the Salvation Army hall in a short while. He asked if he and his nephew could attend or was the meeting just for the soldiers. He was invited and came to the Salvation meeting. The next Sunday morning he arrived in time to attend the Christian Understanding Class where the session was on the subject of how to be sure you are a Christian. In the weeks that followed he attended both the Sunday morning and Sunday night meetings.

During one of the class sessions he told the class the story of his conversion. After the Vietnam War as a wounded veteran he was able to attend Western Michigan State University in Kalamazoo. He had become involved with drugs and alcohol while in the service and was continuing this lifestyle while attending the university. One Saturday afternoon he had decided to drive a young lady to her home in Ann Arbor, Michigan, so he could meet her parents. His real plan was to introduce her to his lifestyle of alcohol and drugs.

While traveling down the highway they noted a sign that said there was a flower show at the Jackson City auditorium. Hoping to kill some time they left the expressway and were soon getting out of their car in the parking lot of the city auditorium. As they walked in through the back door the young man noted that there were no flowers, only people sitting on chairs listening to a group of singers on the stage. They were shown to some empty chairs at the back of the auditorium.

As they sat and listened to the speaker, the young man in his half-drunken stupor realized that it was some sort of religious meeting. He had heard about God as a youth but had no intention of making any changes in what he considered to be the good life. As he listened to the message and the invitation to come forward to give his life to God, he said to himself that this message was not

for him. As they sang the invitation song he held on to his chair.
Then, he said, something seemed to lift him out of his seat. He
found himself walking down the aisle toward the front where he
was greeted by a Christian worker. After some counseling he
prayed and asked God to take over his life.

They gave him some study material and a *Bible*. He took the
young lady to her parents' home and never caused the harm that he
had planned. He returned home and began to study the *Bible* and
the material he had been given by the worker. His craving for
alcohol and drugs never returned. With his college studies and
work, he spent the next three months as a new Christian alone.
The worker had mentioned a church that he should attend, but
because there was no such church in his hometown and he did not
know where to go, he never looked for another church.

One afternoon while he was studying, a knock came at the
door. When he opened it, there stood two young men, with *Bibles*
in hand and friendly smiles on their faces. They introduced
themselves as members of The Church of Jesus Christ of Latter
Day Saints who had come to help him understand the *Bible*. He
welcomed them in as if they were sent from God. He joined their
church and for three and a half years served as their lay youth
leader.

He said in all the years he had been in their church he had not
heard the gospel message until he stopped to listen to that meeting
on the street corner by the ice cream store. He said that he was
sorry that he had lost those years because the wrong people came
to his door. He became a Senior Soldier at the next enrollment and
began to share his faith with his family and friends.

While we were on an overseas assignment, we noted that the
War Cry carried the news that this young man had been made the
corps Evangelism Secretary of the Battle Creek, Michigan, corps.

Life is Not Fair

The phone rang and the voice on the other end of the line said,
"My ex-daughter-in-law just called and sounded like she was

going to commit suicide. Would you talk to her?" It was the Home League treasurer who said her daughter-in-law could see me this afternoon if I had time.

She came in at 4:00 p.m. right from work, dressed in her nurse's uniform. I said before we get started I have something that I would like to share with her, and gave her the *Four Laws Booklet*. When we finished with the prayer of commitment, she smiled and said that was what she needed.

I invited her to our Christian Understanding Class the next Sunday morning. One of the classes she attended was How to Experience God's Love and Forgiveness. She was able to apply those principles to her problem. She and her two daughters attended the Sunday services for the next ten weeks.

I discovered that her husband, who was a high school football coach, had divorced her and moved to Texas with his new wife. He was not sending child support. Every time he came to see his parents she had had him picked up. She had been a nurse in the U. S. Army with the rank of captain. After her husband left her she had been dating a doctor from the hospital where she worked. He had been telling her that he was going to divorce his wife and marry her; but had just told her that he was going to stay with his wife and their plans were off. Like a day on General Hospital she came in to see me on the day that her doctor friend had ended their affair.

As the weeks passed she had a smile on her face. She and her daughters became soldiers in the corps. Her mother-in-law called and said her son had come to town and his ex-wife had not called the police. He said a miracle had taken place--she was like a new person.

Bell Ringers Needed

We had announced our need for Christmas workers at our Ladies Home League meeting. One of our regular senior ladies asked if her husband, who had just retired from the Michigan highway department as a surveying crew chief, could work too.

He came with his wife to an orientation meeting, where we closed the meeting by sharing the "Four Spiritual Laws" which ended with a prayer of commitment to the Christian way of life.

All eight people in the class prayed the prayer. I invited them to attend our Christian Understanding Class the next Sunday. The couple attended all the meetings and came to the class to become soldiers. One of the questions we ask new recruits is, "What church do you belong to?" He said he had been brought up Baptist, but twenty-five years ago he had joined the Jehovah Witness Movement. I asked how long ago he had quit. He said thirteen weeks ago when he came to ring bells. He said for those years he had not been able to find what he was looking for, but had found it the day he prayed that prayer.

He and his wife became uniformed soldiers. He helped teach the new Christian's class and often read the scripture from the pulpit during the Sunday Morning Holiness Meeting. He told all who would listen that we needed to visit door-to-door. They were two of our new sixty-five new soldiers.

CHAPTER FOURTEEN

REPUBLIC DE PANAMA

Some One Needs You!

The phone rang and the voice on the other end said, "You had better sit down! Your request for missionary service has been answered, and you and your wife are going to be assigned to a Spanish speaking country." I reminded him that that request was made five years ago and we had never received an answer. They gave us one year to get ready; we were to attend Spanish classes and tell no one of this assignment.

We went to Territorial Headquarters for testing, and after five hours of testing Dr. Lee Fisher informed us that we should be able to handle whatever assignment we were given. The Spanish classes went well and the year passed quickly. We received a call from the Field Department that our appointment had been changed to the Republic of Panamá where we were to be Divisional Commanders for the next four years.

For some reason our going overseas was never announced by the Army until just before we were to go. We asked if we could stay for the National Congress in St Louis as we had twenty-five soldiers who were attending and four weeks of vacation coming. Our request was denied and our old Corps Sergeant Major from Belmont, Ken Booth and his wife saw us off at the airport.

Republic de Panamá

We flew into Mexico City from Chicago and were met at the airport by the Territorial Commander, Colonel Jacque Eggers, and his wife who took us to lunch and then to their quarters. The next day we toured the Army centers and ended at Territorial

Headquarters where we were introduced to the staff.

The Colonel, who was Swiss and could speak and write in five different languages, reviewed the problems we were to face as the new leaders of Panamá. With the transfer of the Canal Zone to Panamá, the government required that the Army remove all signs, songbooks and *Bibles* in English. The Colonel told us what we should expect to find in every center.

We were informed that all Army buildings were unmarked. There were only a few songbooks in English that had been brought into the country by Majors Bill and Alice in their luggage. Most English *Bibles* were in the hands of the soldiers. Most of the Panamanian populations of West Indian descent owe their presence in the country to the monumental efforts to build the Panama Canal in the late 19th and early 20th centuries.

The Army had been brought over from the Caribbean in 1904 by the U.S. government when the black workers came to help build the canal. Some of the officer staff asked us who we were and why we were given this assignment. As far as they knew we were the first officers who had ever been taken to lunch by the Commander. It should be noted at this time that most command appointments were given not earned.

A Change in the Weather

Mexico City, with its twenty-five million people and smoke-filled air, still has spring-like weather. The General Secretary, who was second in command, boarded Aero-Mexico with us for our flight to Panamá. As we flew over Central America we saw fires burning and thought a revolution had started; instead we were told that it was only the sugarcane fields being prepared for harvest. As we got off the plane into the air-conditioned airport, we were met by Major Inez, the Divisional Secretary, who greeted us and took us to our waiting van. A blast of hot moist air engulfed us as we stepped out of the airport. Our knees buckled. We could have gotten back on the plane and gone home.

As we drove the fifteen miles to our new home, we saw the

poverty of a third world country. The Volkswagen van did not have air-conditioning--there was no escaping the heat. We were told that every day it was 95 degrees in the shade and could get to 120 out in the sun in the afternoon. Fortunately it dropped down to 75 in the evening. Everything shut down between noon and 3 p.m. During the nine wet months of the year there was a rainfall of as much as 435 inches and during the three dry months there was no rain. All nature had adjusted to this climate--only man, which included us, had a tough time surviving.

We discovered that we had a maid and a yardman that the government maintained we must keep employed. Our laundry room was outside next to our welfare center. No water heater was needed because the water from the tap was warm enough to take a shower. Our welfare office and clothing room were on the same lot. Funds from friends allowed us to repair the center that had been gutted by fire. The massive mango tree next door at the headquarters for Standard Oil was the home of a flock of parrots and on occasions the feeding place at night of many large fox bats.

Our residence was on the second floor of Divisional Headquarters. There were five air-conditioners that ran day and night to cool the three bedrooms with fourteen-foot ceilings. I spent four years painting twenty oil paintings to fill the upper walls. Several requests for portraits came from the training college in Chicago, one of which, a picture of a younger Commissioner Norman Marshall, hangs in Marshall Hall. Three portraits of missionary children from Colon were given in memory of Major Colville. We had Army guests from all over the world stay with us.

An Eighteen-Month Year

The Divisional financial books were confused, because they had included eighteen months of income and expense, which allowed them to think that they had had a really good year. This kind of thinking had been prevalent. All officers came in to headquarters on Thursday to pick up their checks and have a meal with the staff. None of the ten centers did their own books or paid any of their bills. Bags of money in the safe had not been recorded.

None of the four other American officers had received a salary for some time and would have resigned and gone home if they had had money for airfare. We asked them to wait several weeks. There were only eight officers for the ten appointments. A married couple received fifty dollars and single officers received thirty dollars a week salary when they could get it. As food from the supermarket was very expensive, we all would buy our food from the street markets.

We closed the books with permission from Headquarters and started with the balances from the bank. During the months that followed all appointments were given their own financial books with Mrs. Anderson conducting bookkeeping classes for every center.

After the headquarters officers left, the previous Divisional Commander showed up and asked if he could see the books to make a few changes. He had been staying downtown with his family at a hotel waiting for a chance to finish his bookwork. We let him do his best not letting him know there was a new set of books. We bid him farewell as he and his family returned to an appointment in England.

Funds were located to pay the officers their back salary, and we convinced them that things would get better. As headquarters said we could set the salary at whatever level we wanted, salaries were raised to one hundred dollars a week for married couples and fifty dollars for single officers. All reinforcement officers received the same salary that the native officers received. No official money came from outside of the country for any officers. At this time money was not being set aside for us to receive when we got back home.

Stand Up When the Commander Arrives.

At our first meeting we were surprised when everyone stood as we entered the chapel, a custom we could never get used to. We were in the presence of the old Army, which was very British. An official U. S. military identification card was given to me by an advisory board member that said, "Major Lester Anderson." He had been given the card by an official from the South Command. It allowed us to eat, for a small cost, at any of the five officer's clubs. Every year I was given a paid membership by a board member for the Rotary Club, which included meals. Papers were given to me to sign that made me president of the Salvation Army in Panama. All property, money and personnel belonged to me and not the international Salvation Army.

We received a call from the American ambassador's office, which told us not to leave our building if there was a "Red Alert." They would send an armored military car to pick us up because I was the president of a company and could be kidnapped and held for ransom. They informed me that I was to serve on the United Nations Committee for Political Refugees for all of South America. One day we were not so important, the next we were too important for our own good. The Divisional Commander in Venezuela, who had the same arrangement, caused many problems when he left and took everything with him.

Centers of Service

From ten centers the Army preached the gospel and served the needy in all of Panama not just the Zone. The Canal Zone had been the Army's home and center of service for seventy-five years, and English had been our language. This bit of America was ten miles wide and little more than forty miles long. All of our centers ran from Panama City and the Pacific Ocean on the south to Colon on the Caribbean to the north. They included seven corps, a school for the adult blind, a Children's Home, and a residence for old men. Three of the corps had feeding centers.

In the 1940s, the Divisional Commander, who was Swedish and didn't have a clear understanding of Spanish or English, had been asked to reregister the Army with the Canal Zone. He went to downtown Panama City and registered the Army as a Panamanian corporation. When the changeover came, some unregistered churches and organizations that were in the Canal Zone were asked to leave the country. We were never questioned.

We needed many more officers to fill our appointments. Thirteen cadets in training in Mexico City would become officers the next year. The centers were as follows: Hogar Jackson (Old Men's Home), Colon 3rd St. Corps, Colon 14th Street Corps, Hogar Dr. Eno in Sabanitas (Girls Home), Chilibe Corps, Paraiso Corps, Panama Central Corps, School for the Blind, Rio Abajo Corps, Welfare and Family Service (at Divisional Headquarters).

Hogar Jackson (Old Men's Home)

Hogar Jackson (the Jackson Home) was named after one of the officers who came over with the West Indians when they came to build the Canal. There were about five hundred Salvation Army families who settled in the Colon area where we set up employment offices, schools, day nurseries and three corps.

After our arrival the Dutch Council was able to obtain $15,000 to repair the roof and paint the entire fifteen-room structure. The men paid a fee for their room which included three meals a day. Many of the men were blind and would have been robbed if they stepped out onto the street. The officer family of five lived on the second floor. Meals were served to poor children in the neighborhood, and many families came to get drinking water when their water was shut off.

Colon Third Street Corps

Nine months of the year Colon had three to four inches of rain a day which made the open street sewers work. During the dry season our eyes would water as we walked down the street. Colon was one of the original three corps. While visiting the corps we noticed a piano at the back of the hall and asked who played their piano. One of the soldiers remarked that it didn't work because it had been destroyed by termites, but they kept it so they could tell everyone they had a piano. One day the officer went out visiting and forgot to lock the door to his apartment, and when he returned home all his furniture and personal items were missing.

While conducting a Sunday Morning Holiness meeting one of the soldiers looked at our songbooks and remarked how much she wished she had one. The corps had only one songbook. She said the one she had was taken away by the government.

You Can Have Your English Books

We checked with the new government and discovered that they had rescinded the order against English in our meetings. Religious services could be conducted in English as long as we used Spanish in part of the service. Our buildings could be marked as long as we used both Spanish and English. We contacted the Army songbook sellers and were informed that the books were out of print and it would be months before we could get new ones. We needed five hundred song books. The post office informed us that the duty on each new book would be about $8, but used book could come in duty free. The new census report came out and showed that the Army had over eight hundred registered adult church members in Panama.

English and Spanish *Bibles* were available from the Gideons at no cost to us. The only used Army songbooks that we could think of were those we had seen at the back of most corps chapels in the United States used only when they had an overflow crowd. Most of them needed some repair but were useable. As only one or two could be sent at a time, we would need to ask for more than 250 corps to send used books.

We thought of our friends back in the states, and asked some Divisional Commanders we knew to ask their corps to send us one or two used songbooks. We suggested that they have a prayer service over the used books and have the soldiers sign their names so the soldiers who received the book would know who cared about them. It would also show the post office that they were used books. We sent the letters and waited. More than five hundred songbooks began to arrive with wonderful words of dedication. Most of them thanked us for the opportunity. The books were let into the country duty free. We rejoiced at God's goodness.

Colon 14th Street Corps

This corps was the bigger of the two. The Rainbow Corps had been united with the 14th Street when their area was closed. There was a large Home League, an active children's program, and two hundred very poor families were fed each week. Bamboo Lane, a notorious drug district, ran behind the building. The Dennie, Panama's undercover police, would shoot the drug dealers on the spot when they tried to sell them drugs.

While visiting the officer we heard gunfire and thought it was a car backfiring. When we looked out from the second floor, we saw two men come from the alley with guns in hand and get into their car. Another man came out and fell on the street. Several friends came and picked him up, put him in their car and drove toward the hospital. There were few drug problems in Colon and all of Panama.

The old city had been built when the French had attempted to build the Canal. The population of 150,000 was West Indian with 65 percent unemployment. The Free Zone employed about 5,000, and the only other employers were the Canal, shipping and the U.S. military. There was often a warm bed situation where every bed in the house had someone sleeping in it 24/7. All police traveled in twos and would keep eye contact with other police. There was a protected area for those disembarking from the cruise ships.

Three blocks from the Colon 14th St. Corps

Football Giant

A very large black man with his wife and child came into our office. He and his wife were from America and had been visiting in Colon when they were approached by two men who demanded their money. As a football player he had feared no man and these men looked like no match for him.

They grabbed his baby from his wife and put a knife to her throat. He said he cried like a baby and gave them every thing they had. What was he to do? We called the American Consulate and they sent a car to pick them up and provided money, a hotel room, and an air ticket back to the states. The only place he could think of when he was in need was the Army.

Major Colville Died Suddenly

The Corps Officer, Major Colville, died suddenly, and over four hundred people showed up for her funeral. Seventeen pastors on the platform wanted to take part in the service. We marched the eight blocks from the corps building to the cemetery with two bands and two hundred ladies with white Salvation Army style hats. We did a short committal service and departed while the officers and friends sang and waited for the burial marker to be posted. We discovered that many of her friends waited to see the grave numbers--because she was such a good person, they bet the number in the national lottery the next day and it was a winner. We spoke out against the lottery.

The New Officers

We appointed Captain and Mrs. Santana, who had four children, as corps officers. They were good, kind people who spoke only Spanish. The first Sunday we discovered that all the pictures of Christ along with the cross and others pictures were gone. When we asked him where they had gone, he told us that they were graven images and had no place in the house of God. I asked him to save all of them for the next officers which he did. Most of the older soldiers could understand some Spanish but spoke mostly English; the young could speak and write Spanish and only speak English, and some of the little children only spoke Spanish.

The Canadians Do Good Work

The Canadian counsel was able to obtain a gift of $140,000 to repair the Colon 14th Street building. The check came within weeks and was put into an account that earned 17 per cent interest. The Canadian counsel was able to buy a new diesel fifteen-passenger van for $30,000 for the corps and the Children's Home.

The Canadian counsel, who served with her husband on our Advisory Board, asked if we would speak with their director of projects from Costa Rica. When she came to see us, she said she needed to spend funds that were directed by her government to fight communism in Central America some of which could be given to the Army for capital repairs.

What she didn't spend before the end of the year, she was required to send back. As we went from place to place, she would ask how much I thought the repairs would cost, and write out a check and hand it to me. When I asked if she needed a receipt, she said no, and if I needed more I should let her know. She gave funds to repair the roof, fence, and road to our children's home and also bought a new diesel truck for our Men's Social clothing room pick up.

Hogar Dr. Eno Sabanitas (Girls' Home)

Sabanitas was a little village up the mountain south of Colon where a Dr. Eno had donated his home to be used as a girl's home. When we arrive there were thirty-six children of different ages and only two workers taking care of the home. There were four boys who along with their sister had been willed to the Army upon the death of their mother because she did not want her daughter to be sold into child prostitution by her family. The court had ruled that we must take them. One of the corps officers took the boys until a home could be found for them.

The property included seventeen hectors of jungle that went from the main road to the Panama Canal. The girls were sent to us by the court, and most of them stayed with us until they were eighteen. The water had not worked for months and the local fire department would come with their truck and fill our large water tank. After we were there for several years, a crew who were repairing the main road came to the door and asked if we wanted our water turned on. It seems that years before someone who was repairing the road had turned it off and forgotten to turn it back on.

Cats in the House

When new lieutenants arrived, they told us in Spanish that they had "gatos" (cats) coming in through the iron bar doors at night. I told them that it would be no problem, just don't feed them. They said, "No, no, they are, "trigrus." They were big jungle cats, ocelots. We had mesh installed which kept them out.

The girls and the officers slept upstairs behind locked doors. When the officers showed us where they slept, we were moved to provide more help. One had a small room with just a cot and a dresser; the other slept on a cot in a room with three or four babies. Several times the downstairs was broken into at night and everything of value removed.

This home was a work of faith. When we needed appliances, they would arrive in an unmarked truck with an installer, with no indication of where they came from. Food was delivered in the same manner. We thought it probably was from the military officers' wives. On an unannounced visit the government gave us a top rating for having the happiest children.

Baby Needs Shoes

Most of the girls had only one or two changes of clothes; when school started, they all needed uniforms. There was no money for shoes, but a Jewish shoemaker said if we would have the girls stand on a piece of paper with their name on it and draw their feet he would make each of them a pair of school shoes. Within a week we received all the shoes at no cost. As the military wives were not allowed to give new items to the girls, many of the clothing items were washed before they came to the home.

$1.95 a Week

We reviewed the Girl's Home accounts and discovered we were only spending $1.95 a week to feed each girl. The staff went into the city markets every week and asked for fruit, vegetables and meat. Donations came in from friends in the States.

A visitor who wanted to do something good for several older girls slipped them money to buy some personal items. The next morning they were gone having taken the evening bus into the big city and back into street prostitution. They had been placed in our custody by the courts. We tried to find them but they were gone from us; the courts sent us three more to take their place.

Up the Mountains to Chilibe

We had a visit from Commissioner and Mrs. Richard Holz, leaders of the Central Territory, to conduct a Mini-congress. They were doing Sunday meetings at Colon in the morning and Panama Central in the evening. We had stopped to visit the girls at Dr. Eno Home and were passing by the Chilibe Corps building that was a pole barn with a tin roof, without water or electricity. The soldiers would chase the snakes from under the platform before each meeting. We had told the lady Captain that because of the heat she

should not expect the Holts to stop. A large crowd was in front of
the building waving as we went by leading the Commissioner to
say we must turn around and go back for a visit.

During the meeting the Holts sang and gave a short message.
As we drove away, he said something must be done for these
people and asked what a building would cost. We had been told
that $50,000 would be needed if we used a native contractor where
we could get the material at 50 percent of cost. A check arrived
and in less than a year we had a building that held up to three
hundred people for the dedication.

Visit Every Family in Sight of the Building

All of the corps conducted a visitation program. The officers
from the division came on Saturday and conducted a street meeting
and visited homes nearby. In Chilibe Captain Mini Soto and her
soldiers visited over two hundred homes. When the priest and

nuns discovered what had been done, they went door to door and told the people that the Army was not a church. All but one family, the Jehovah Witnesses who lived on the hill above the corps, said they attended the corps.

Many of the soldiers came from back in the jungle. After one evening service a uniformed soldier left his wife and children with his daughter who lived across the road from the corps. He was walking home the five miles in the dark to save his property from his neighbors. When I asked if he had a flashlight, he said that he planned to walk in the moonlight. One of our members had gone to check his bed of ornamental plants down by the river before going to work. When they looked for him, they found that he had been killed by a bushmaster snake. He had a wife and four children who attended the corps.

Night in the Jungle

We often drove our guests through the jungle after dark. To drive from Colon to the city of Panama took as much as an hour and a half. The sun set a 6:30 p.m. year round and we would plan to get to a small park along the road in the jungle just as it was getting dark.

We would sit with our windows rolled down and wait for the night creatures to come alive. As we listened the drums would roll, the horns would beep, the marimbas would bonk, and we might even hear a low growl. In a short time our guests wanted to escape back to the city lights. In the daylight there were bugs, frogs, birds, monkeys, snakes, land crabs and other small harmless critters that owned the forest. The land crabs, red or orange and as big as a dinner plate, live in the jungle and often cross the roads in front of cars with their pinchers raised. They hold their snappers above their heads and seem to say, "Catch me if you can!"

Paraiso Corps

The city of Paraiso was founded during Panama's Spanish colonial era; the area around Paraiso was a stop on the overland route between the Atlantic and the Pacific. It was visited mostly during the isthmus' dry season; it was said that from the hill overlooking Paraiso, the tower of old Panama City's cathedral, eight miles away, could be seen on a clear day.

In the 1850s, Paraiso was made a rail stop on the Panama Railroad, though it was little more than a village with an exceptional natural spring. In 1882, when the French Canal Company began work, Paraiso was the southernmost point of French dry season excavation effort. Dumping cars continued to carry soil out of the area for years, though by the end of the 19th century, canal works were little more than a token effort and the population of Paraiso was about eight hundred, living in one hundred frame houses and one hundred huts.

The corps and Ladies Home League was attended by about twenty people. The hall was up-to-date and the residence was adequate for a small family. The officer in charge of our new Men's Social lived here for several years. The corps is now closed. The train doesn't stop there anymore.

Panama Central Corps

This corps, with a chapel that would hold over two hundred people, was in the center of the city of Panama, three blocks from the bay and the Pacific Ocean. It had a grand piano and was the corps where special international guests would speak. Twenty of the senior ladies played their tambourines at the same time on most Sunday nights. The smell of the street coming through the barred windows along with rather large winged cockroaches made for interesting meetings.

There was no air conditioning in any of our corps buildings, instead the chapel had low ceiling fans. During General Jarl Walhstrum's visit one of the officers grabbed the Army flag intending to lead a march of praise around the hall. He swung the flag into the whirling fan; broken parts flew around the chapel without hurting anyone.

Many times our visitors, who were not accustomed to the heat, would fall asleep. On one occasion our famous guest pianist dozed off and had to be awakened to perform his number.

Betty Anderson, Colonal John Bate, Lester Anderson, Mrs. Walhstrum and General Walhstrum

A Blind Ghost

The school for the blind was held at the Panama Central Corps each week. The new building was surrounded by the old city in an area where there had been families of thieves who the government had moved to the suburbs to a village called Samaria. The robbers were feared because they were also killers. Some of our blind students lived in their area.

When one of our older blind students died, a busload of

Samarians arrived and filled up one side of the chapel; some present who knew who they were got up and left. As the dead were frozen, when you looked in through a small window in the coffin their face seemed blue and covered with what looked like sweat. The coffins were used many times. The poor were dropped into a common grave with up to fifty other corpses.

When the service ended some of the thieves came forward to the coffin and lifted the lid, dropped a roll of red string at the feet of the corpse. Someone went to stop them, but the mortician said they were doing no harm and to let them finish. One of the thieves had taken the blind man's money and feared that his ghost would come and follow him around for the rest of his life.

Heat on the Street

A group of officers and soldiers had gone downtown to do a street service in the early afternoon. Large crowds passed by, and many stopped to listen to the songs, many of which were sung in Spanish. It came time to sing choruses without the band, and I put on my small accordion and began to play for the singers. The sun was very hot. I began to hear a clinking sound. My music was going away. Soon the keys stopped working. The sun had melted the bee's wax that held the bass reeds which kept dropping somewhere inside the accordion. Later I discovered it could not be repaired.

From that time on I played my mandolin in the meetings. When we got back to the States, one of the soldiers asked if I could use a small accordion that only needed straps and a case. It was new and was the best brand on the market. God was still taking care of us.

Amelia de Castro School for the Blind

Two blind Jewish sisters had founded a school for the adult blind to which Helen Keller had come for the opening. A framed letter signed by her hung on the wall for all to see. The sisters passed away and willed the school to the Salvation Army. When we arrived there were two well trained teachers both blind. The students received a meal and help living a near normal life. The national lottery gave each blind person $150 in tickets, which they could sell and keep the money. Many people thought they could win if they purchased one of their tickets.

They also could work counting money, loved to sing and put on programs, and we took them on trips around the country. The older students helped the younger. One way they made money was making fold-away shopping bags from fish nets.

The Jewish community supported this school with an annual drive. In the mid-1990s an estimated seven thousand Jews lived in Panama, including one thousand Israelis, mostly in Panama City, but there are also communities in Colon, David and the former American Canal Zone. Most Jews in Panama are traditional in their Jewish practices.

Eleven Jewish men served on our National Advisory Board, second only to the Greek community as supporters. We were expected to attend their funerals and other special events in our full white uniforms. Many times we were the only gentiles amidst hundreds of Jews. Funerals were times of feasting, with the finest of foods served in abundance.

Blind Bus Driver

A blind man came off the street to ask if he could come to our dinner for the blind. Someone down at the central city park, where he was living under a park bench, had told him to go to the Salvation Army for help. He told us that he had been a bus driver and suddenly without warning his right eye had gone blind. He pulled the bus over and called for help. The doctor told him that he had a detached retina and should expect the other eye to go. He got a job driving a cab. Several months later his other eye went blind. He pulled over his cab and again got help. After several months of blindness his wife and family dropped him off at the park and drove away.

He asked the people who ate their lunches in the park for food, went to the Laundromat and hid in the bathroom where he asked the ladies to wash and dry his one set of clothing. He had also discovered that he had an inoperable cancer. One of our rich Dutch volunteers said she would pay for him to enter our old men's home in Colon. She bought him new clothing and saw that he was looked after until his death. We made room for him and he spent his last year in the safety of our home.

People Give Things to the Salvation Army

A Car

As the Divisional Commanders we had been given a small car without air conditioning. A lady with her helper came into our welfare office wanting to give us a box of old things that were worn out, and she asked for a receipt for the full amount of new clothing. American citizens could give to the Panama Salvation Army and take their donation as a tax deduction. When Mrs. Anderson informed her that that was not the way it was done, she went away in a huff.

Several weeks later she returned and said she wanted to give us a car. Mrs. Anderson went out expecting to look at an old car, and quickly came back in and said you must see this. The lady was giving us a new fully equipped "K" car with 900 miles on the odometer. We discovered that she was heir to the largest wine company in Panama, whose husband had died and she was moving back to the States. We gave our little white car to the Divisional Secretary, and spent the next two years driving that very fine air conditioned gift from God.

A Hospital

The plastic surgeon for the Baptist Hospital on the Kuna Isle of Gundie was leaving after working among the Kuna children repairing cleft lips for more than twenty-five years. One of the world's top plastic surgeons, he had no money and no property and had been offered a contract in an Arab country. They wanted us to take over this twenty-bed hospital which headquarters said we should look at and get back to them.

I boarded a small plane with the mail and medicine for the Kuna Islands. The pilot, who worked as a comptroller for the U.S. Air Force during the week, had become a missionary bush pilot on weekends. The co-pilot was older, had a patch over one eye and limped. The other passenger was a Baptist minister. I had been told not to eat the fish under any circumstances and to bring fifty dollars in small bills because as we went through the village they would offer handmade items for sale.

After an hour in the air I asked the pilot how long before we would reach our destination. As I looked down over the forest he said, "Another hour and a half." The copilot pointed to an opening in the distance and said, "That is the spot where we crashed. I was the only one to live. I walked out. I lost an eye and a leg." I scrunched down in my seat and prayed. After what seemed like hours, we reached our destination, a very small gravel road. The pilot dipped his wing and we saw a dugout canoe coming toward the road. We had arrived.

Three thousand Kuna live around the hospital in bamboo huts with thatched roofs with smoke filling the air. We melted in the heat. The hospital was small with a water system heated by solar heat. There was a small food bar where they sold meals to visitors. I had a hot dog with chips. No fish. My guide said the small buildings built out over the water were their bathrooms.

After we inspected the hospital, we toured the island. Because I was in uniform, they flocked around trying to sell molas and other items. I had done a little reading about their crafts, and spent most of my money. As we neared time to depart, I saw a young lady wearing what I considered to be the best mola on the island. I made an offer of fifteen dollars. She went into her hut and came out wearing a different one. I took the blouse and started toward the dock. An old man came out of his hut with a doll of a lady, hand carved out of dark wood, with a fish in her hand. I only had eight dollars which he took. The guide said I had done real well having purchased two treasures. The mola was top grade and worth on the market about six hundred dollars. The doll was a national treasure and beyond price. We departed in the late afternoon and arrived back home as the sun was setting. I thanked God for the safe journey and told the preacher that I didn't think we would take the hospital.

A Compound

The phone rang and the voice on the other end said, "We want to give you our village." There were fifteen homes, an assembly hall, and office and a chapel in a fenced area high in the mountains. It was the Wycliffe Translators' compound. One of their pilots had discovered a cluster of new buildings in a clearing back in the jungle and given their location to the CIA. What they had discovered was a drug manufacturing camp being run by Noriega's men. As a result the Wycliffe staff had all their visas recalled and were ordered to leave the country. They told me that it would be our property until they returned. If they couldn't get back in, it would be ours. In three months we welcomed them back.

Five Churches

The Methodist church was cutting off support for their West Indians' native churches. Some of the pastors contacted us and wanted their church to join the Salvation Army. I flew to the city of David and inspected a church, which was old and deeply in debt. The pastor seemed to be having a problem with boys, and I was advised by a Methodist friend not to take the churches. I never called Headquarters. All the churches were closed.

Colombia

Seven of our officers were from Colombia. The relationships between Panamanians and Colombians were very good. The Army had had a corps there but it had been closed many years ago. We had a steady flow of applicants from Colombia for officership. A Louise Lupera had started a work in Medellin, a city of three million high in the Andes, infamous for being the home of a drug cartel. He wanted us to come and see his Salvation Army.

As the Territorial Commander said London wanted to reopen the corps, four male officers went with me for a four-day trip to visit Louise and to prepare the paperwork so the Army could return to Colombia. Louise had been a Captain in the Colombian military. He had been the head of security at their international airport, but resigned when the drug dealers moved in. He had a large grown family, including his married children living in his home. He had about sixty members attending his corps. Today there is a children's care center, clinic and dispensary, feeding centers, and a corps in Medellin.

No Caps Please

As we were leaving the hotel on our second day, the manager stopped us at the door to tell us not to wear our Salvation Army caps as they were shooting men with military hats today. After a day spent inspecting buildings for our corps opening he informed us on our return three men with military caps had been killed. We returned home to the safety of Panama.

Rio Abajo Corps

The Down River Corps in a better section of the Panama City, had a kindergarten, an adult training center, and an active youth corps. Our water bill was very high, but we could find no water leak. Someone suggested that we turn off the water in the training center. When it was turned off, we noted that the neighbors down the block came out to see what was wrong. We discovered that when the plumbing was being changed, someone had hooked all the houses to our water system providing water to ten houses. The city came and made some changes which cut our water bill to 10 percent of what we had been paying.

Up The River Without Water

The male officers gathered for a three-hour trip up the Chepo River to do open-air meetings in the Darien jungle. There is an estimated population of fifteen thousand Chocó Indians who live along the banks of this river. As the tide went up in the bay of Panama, the Chepo River rose with the tide. We took a large dugout canoe with a guide, making five stops with many people coming to hear our small band and the gospel preached in Spanish.

We ended up thirty miles back in the jungle where the trees, exotic birds, flowers, monkeys, bamboo huts and the river made it an event to remember. Our guide told us there were no roads, plumbing, or electric lights in this area. When the water stopped coming, we turned around and spent three hours going back to civilization.

When we stopped to eat and wait for our guide, this talking parrot greeted us in Spanish. He sat at the end of the table waiting for us to feed him. The Spanish speaking officers said he used mostly swear words.

A Day in the Real Jungle

My brother Dr. Wayne Anderson was spending a month with us and wanted to visit the real jungle. Gatun Lake was made to make it possible for the ships to go from the Pacific to the Caribbean. The island of Barro Colorado in the center of the lake has been a protected area and a jungle study center for the Smithsonian institute. It was open to five persons from outside the scientific community one day a week with permission given by the American embassy. We called and got two passes, arrived early in the morning by train and took the antiquated boat out to the island.

We climbed the hill to the research station and were told where to go and what to look out for. The biggest problem was biting insets. We saw groups of monkeys, bird-eating spiders, butterflies, and exotic birds. We climbed high into the forest on the twenty-four-story scaffolding used by the scientist to study butterflies and birds, stopped to hear the holler monkey do his thing and heard large animals crashing through the bushes--probably tapirs that were in the area. We ended our day and boarded the train back to La Boca.

The Archbishop

Archbishop Marcos McGrath, who was six-foot-six and spoke perfect English and Spanish, asked me to join with the leaders of the country as part of the welcome party for Pope John Paul II the next Saturday. As part of the United Nations Committee for Political Refuges for South America I met with the Archbishop on a regular basis. Of the five members of the committee three of us were pro-American.

The other two bishops supported the Sandinistas and Cubans, and sided with the communists who had been expelled from Chili and came to Panama. They controlled the compound and made it impossible for ex-communists to find a safe place to hide. We were glad to turn the project over to the government of Panama when the compound got out of our control.

McGrath was on the board for Notre Dame in South Bend, Indiana, and had eight bishops under his jurisdiction. He was the bishop who tried to get Noriega to surrender peacefully. When the Pope arrived at the airport over one hundred fifty thousand Panamanians were there to greet him. We were asked to lock arms and stand as a fence of protection as we welcomed him to Panama. The bishop next to me reached out his hand to the Pope, and thousands of Catholics came through the opening. The Pope raised his hands and as he turned his bodyguards filled in behind him. Over four hundred thousand people showed up the next day in a large field for his message and blessing.

White Uniforms

We were given matching white uniforms from the family of Commissioner Clyde J. Cox who had them made for their visit to the tropics. They fit both of us without alterations; all we had to do was changed the trim to Majors. We wore these uniforms for special occasions looking like the captains of the Love Boat. At our headquarters we had our own supplies and purchasing department. Most of our hats and pins came from Hong Kong; our uniforms were made locally. The officers wore a white shirt or blouse with red applets, which it was often necessary to change three times a day because of the extreme heat.

There was a blue fly that laid its eggs on white garments that were hung out of doors. Because the worm would get under your skin and caused elephantiasis, our maid ironed all of our white clothing daily to kill them. A blue fly bit my arm and laid an egg under my skin. I shaved the hair off my arm and painted the area with clear fingernail polish; however the worm grew and it became necessary for a doctor to remove it. The doctor said I had done the right thing

Marcos

Marcos, working at a downtown bank, had gone out for a lunch break. As he passed a Salvation Army street meeting, he noticed that the speaker was one of his old high school teachers. She was in uniform and talked about following Jesus. He asked her about the Army and started to visit the Central Corps, leading him to become a member and follow the call to officership.

ST. FRANCIS of ASSISI

He told the story of his time as a Catholic priest in Rome where he traveled with the Pope for several years. After five years he returned to Panama and served in the priesthood. He said while he was cleaning statues in the garden, he realized this was not his calling. His grandmother, who was Chinese and owned the Yellow Cab Company and several buildings in the downtown area, had sent him to the best schools in the city. The Methodist Church operated the best high school which he attended. He had become a believer in their teaching about Jesus.

Skilled in languages he spoke and wrote Chinese, German,

Spanish, and English, and could also read and translate Greek. The paperwork for the new opening in Columbia was done under his direction. Having relatives in most government offices allowed him to give us special service. He and his wife are presently serving as Majors in Mexico.

Alfredo

Alfredo, a tall good looking West Indian who had been raised on the streets of the old city, was our yard man during our four years in Panama. When my brother wanted to go to the dog races, Alfredo went with him. My brother gave him money to bet, but each time he put it in his pocket.

Another time he came to our door and told us we were in trouble. Someone had put a hex, the voodoo symbol for death, on one of our three Royal Palm trees. Mrs. Anderson helped him paint over it with whitewash. When killer bees built a nest in one of our bushes, he knew what to do. He built a fire to smoke them out causing them to sting his face so that he could not see for several hours.

As part of his pay we gave him bags of canned goods that he gave to his mother, who lived somewhere in the old city. One day he called and said he was in jail. The police had arrested him for stealing the groceries and wanted fifteen dollars to bail him out. One of our officers went and paid the money. Two days later he called and said that he was in jail for swearing at a street prostitute. They wanted fifteen dollars to let him go. I told him to tell the police we didn't want him back. He showed up at the office within the hour; they didn't want him either. Once we refused to pay they didn't pick him up again.

General Walhstrum was preaching at a street meeting in downtown Panama City with hundreds of people listening. It was starting to get dark. When the invitation was given to come to the drum head and get saved, no one came forward. Another verse of song was sung. Would the General go without one convert during his first visit to the tropics? From out of the crowd of listeners stepped a tall black man. There was little light and we couldn't tell who it was. Officers gathered around him and prayed. In a few minutes he arose with a big smile on his face. Alfredo had saved the day--the General had his convert.

Noriega

General Noriega was the product of bad politics. When a dictator needed an army to enforce his laws on the people of a country, he sent his men into the backcountry to recruit uneducated boys from the villages to serve as soldiers. They would pay the family one hundred dollars a month and the young man would receive the same. They told the young recruit when he got to camp that he must do everything he was told to do or he and his parents would be killed. Most of them had little education including Noriega. History shows that no one knows when or where Noriega was born in Panama.

The dictator's office called and said he wanted me to come to his home for dinner. When I arrived all the bishops were there. They sat me at the right end of the head table with the dictator, probably because of my white uniform; General Noriega sat at the other end. We studied each other during the entire meeting. I don't think he knew what I was. Men with guns stood at the four corners of the room. Peredas told us of his conversion while watching Jimmy Swagger on television. As a born again Christian he was going to run for president of the country. I think he wanted our support. He ran and lost. Noriega refused to give back his dictatorship as he had agreed before the election. History tells the rest of the story.

One Hundred Dollar Churches

The Church of the Foursquare Gospel and the Church of God had both opened *Bible* colleges in Panama. They trained their native pastors for three months. They were trained to open churches in the bush where the weather made it possible to have an out-of-doors church. One of their American churches would send the pastor one hundred dollars a month if he opened a church and maintained a congregation. A church leader would come by to be sure he was telling the truth. These missions devastated the Catholic churches where they had people, but where there were no priests.

These *Bible* colleges together were putting out about two hundred churches a year; creating new churches everywhere. These denominations were Pentecostal and were anti-Catholic in their teaching. When the Pentecostal churches united for a rally at Panama's largest baseball stadium and invited local pastors, in the spirit of unity, to sit on the platform, Archbishop McGrath showed up in full regalia. The visiting speaker had to change his message. During the four years we were there some of these pastors wanted to start a Salvation Army church in the mountains. They had little or no education and in most cases had been dropped by their American churches.

Our Days in Panama Ended

When we had arrived, we had been told the day that we would be leaving. We were asked three times if we wanted to stay, but we declined the offer for health and family reasons. There were now thirty-four officers and dependents in our appointments. All beds in all quarters were filled. Paperwork for the opening of Colombia had been sent to Headquarters. All buildings that needed repair had been taken care of. A considerable amount of funds were in reserve. We were now the Panamanian Salvation Army.

CHAPTER FIFTEEN

Welcome Home

We arrived back in Chicago, and immediately took our allotted two-month furlough which all Army missionary officers were given after four years of overseas service. We were loaned a car by a caring divisional commander and spent the time visiting friends and relations we had not seen for many years. We had been cautioned by other returned officers to insist on no appointments until after the furlough. They had had a very difficult time adjusting to the return home with no time off and an appointment that required them to go to work the next week.

Oklahoma City Commanders

We were appointed to open the city command in Oklahoma City, Oklahoma, in the Southern Territory a wonderful city that had a great expression of Army activity. Managed by the Army were seventeen senior high-rises, a large daycare program, an active corps, a men's lodge program, a family center, and welfare offices with a total of two hundred fifty six employees. In those days I had to sign all the checks individually.

An active Men's Adult Rehabilitation Center had over a hundred men in the program. Divisional Headquarters for Oklahoma and Arkansas were located in the north of the city.

We had inherited our City Command budget, staff and building from the Divisional Command and were the first city commanders. They let us know that we were not the ones they had planned for and that the Territorial Commander Andrew S. Miller had sent us over their wishes. We tried to make few changes and worked at creating a favorable atmosphere for growth. Headquarters wanted us to correct some of their mistakes. It appeared to us that there were problems that they had been unwilling to correct during their time in charge of the city.

Christmas Downtown

The city had been in a depressed condition because of the oil market. Twenty five percent of the city's office space sat empty. Long standing companies were going broke. As it was obvious we needed a big Christmas effort, I contacted the mayor's office about a Salvation Army Tree of Lights in the downtown area. He thanked me for asking and said he wanted us to take over the Mayor's Tree in the downtown square where they would provide the tree, lights and maintenance for the Christmas season. We told him what we needed and he took care of us. The divisional band and leaders showed up for the lighting, and most of the television stations put us on the evening news.

We contacted all the media to tell them that we would keep them informed on a daily basis. With their support we raised more than had been raised the year before. Since the person ordering our toys had mistakenly made a double order, we had an abundance of blessings for the Christmas season.

The New Corps

The new corps building had been built on a donated piece of land on the far southeast corner of the city. On our first Sunday at the new corps we met old friends. A Sergeant Gene Talkon, who had been a Sunday school member in my first class forty years before, came to the corps with his family. A sergeant Ottly, who had been one of my Junior Soldiers in St. Paul, Minnesota, thirty-five years before, attended with his family. It was like old home week. The soldiers and families at the corps provided a wonderful center of worship.

Rotary Club Award

The Oklahoma City Rotary Club was the home of most of the power in the city. The weekly meeting had been moved to a new location for a special presentation. When I was dropped off at the front door, I told the driver that I would call when the meeting was over. I checked in at the front desk and entered the hall to find that all tables were filled. The mayor and the governor were sitting with the club leaders on the raised platform. Everyone stood for prayer and the pledge of allegiance to the flag.

I noticed that there was a table to the right of the speaker off the platform where only two men were sitting. They motioned for me to come and sit down. I introduced myself and sat down.

Dinner was served and I struck up a conversation with the older man sitting next to me who said he liked the Salvation Army. When I told him about my years in Panama, he told me about his years of exploration as an engineer in the jungles of South America. After almost two years in the wilderness he had come to Colon to stay at the Washington Hotel before returning home to Oklahoma. He remembered the air-conditioning and the best ice cream sundae he had ever had.

The man who had been sitting with us went to the microphone and began to speak about the special award the guest was to receive. He called for Mr. Robert S. Kerr Jr., son of the founder of Kerr McGee Oil, Gas and Uranium Company and head of the Kerr Foundation, to come forward to receive the highest award given by the Rotary Club. The old man setting next to me got up and moved toward the platform. The audience of over five hundred business leaders rose and gave him a thunderous applause. Rotary has always been a good place to meet important people.

Oklahoma City Advisory Board

The Salvation Army in most locations has a board of local leaders who advise us about the needs of the community. Most of the leaders of the city were represented on the wonderful board that was given by the division to the City Command.

Off to the Little Rock Command

After opening the command in Oklahoma City we were sent to work in Little Rock, Arkansas, as Area Commanders. We were located a few blocks from the capitol building and downtown Little Rock. There were three corps, an Adult Rehabilitation Center, a lodge, welfare offices and command center along with an outstanding Women's Auxiliary of over two hundred members who helped support our programs.

Fashion Show at the State House

Hillary Clinton, a member of our auxiliary in good standing, held a fashion show and tea with cookies at the governor's mansion. We arrived early and were greeted by security. They had set up for the program in their front room with all the silver from the battleship USS Arkansas on display. Chelsea came home from school and was introduced to those who were setting up. The ladies arrived and the show went on. Much of the money in the state was in the hands of these ladies.

White Water

Things began to move for the Clintons while we were there. Our advisory board was divided between parties and told us of many of the problems. We went out to see the project known as White Water, fields of weeds and streets without houses. There were suggestions that we should not put any of our money in certain savings and loan companies. Headquarters sent us official papers that needed the signature of the governor. When the Governor signed the papers, I got in the picture. Clinton dressed and looked like a movie star. When I got back to the office, I told the staff that I thought I had met the future president of the United

States. The officers we followed were friends of the Clintons and were present at their inauguration.

Starting the Street People Craze

A speaker at the Downtown Rotary Club informed us that the federal government was closing the local adult care house. The 135 residents that had been placed there by the courts for their protection were to receive a monthly check and with that they had the right to move out on their own. She said that all but thirty were out on the street leaving her with a large building and fifteen of her former employees. Thirty of the new street people showed up at our lodge looking for help while others had moved in under the bridge and were living in boxes and makeshift shacks.

Over the years an industry has risen to take care of these helpless people. Politicians who made this possible have worked this problem for more votes. Most of the street people would be helped if they were institutionalized like they had been in the past. One city has solved their problem by giving the homeless a carton of cigarettes for every week they stayed at the city homeless shelter.

Sixty-Foot Tree of Lights

The chairman of our board owned the CBS radio and television stations for central Arkansas. He wanted to help us as much as he could and arranged to do the 10:30 p.m. weather report live from our Tree of Lights. I had to report eighteen nights from the foot of the very large tree. The city street department came to change the lights for us. We reached our goal and helped over three thousand five hundred families in the Greater Little Rock Area.

Blonde Bell Ringer

Greater Little Rock with a population of around 500,000 was the center of big events for Wal-Mart.   Sam Walton held his annuals awards dinner for his managers in a large downtown hotel and had opened his second Sam's Club in North Little Rock.

We had fifty Christmas kettle sites to fill. We sent a very nice looking young blond lady, who unknown to us was handicapped, to the new Sam's opening.   She smiled and looked very nice but could not read.   While she was on her bathroom break, someone took her kettle.   When she returned she broke down and cried.   Not knowing what to do because she couldn't read the instructions, she called the police.

When the local police arrived, so did a reporter from the Associated Press.   By the time the management of Sam's Club heard, the story had hit the national news.   At the request of management we put another worker there, but sent the young lady back the next week.

The next day we were called to come to the Sam's Club office where they wanted to make sure that we would not remove the Christmas stand.   They had discovered from their security video that the theft appeared to have been done by two new boys on their staff; the kettle and money were returned along with three hundred dollars in cash that someone from the head office said we should have for our trouble.

Sam's Story

Sam and his wife were honored at an evening Rotary meeting that was attended by most of the Little Rock leaders. We attended and sat at a table just to the left of the speaker. Sam knew almost everyone in the building. He told how he had had a strip mall in South Little Rock, and one of his friends in the audience had built a larger mall across the street and put him out of business. He told how he had gone back up home and purchased some Grant stores where he applied some new ideas. He said we knew the rest of the story and thanked those friends who had put him out of business.

Off To Territorial Headquarters in Atlanta

Commissioner Andrew Miller informed us that he wanted us to come to Atlanta to run the new National Conference Center. We were to be the directors in training. Honored by his confidence in us we made the move. We both enrolled in college and were assigned to stay for the summer at the School for Officers Training. Eventually we moved into the residence of the retiring territorial auditor.

The new conference center of which we were to be directors was being constructed. We were welcomed and introduced as the new directors. Headquarters gave us two cars and an expense account. I attended Georgia State University in downtown Atlanta near the office of the Adult Rehabilitation Center where we were to be helpers. Betty attended Decatur College and worked in the bookkeeping department at the center. It was the first time in my life I had ever made the dean's list. As a 54-year-old student I was older than most of my teachers.

It's the Law

One of the important classes that I needed for my new assignment was Georgia State commercial law. The class was being taught by a retired Army colonel, a Georgia lawyer. We met for three hours, three days a week for six weeks. He was interesting and told many stories. Law after law was examined and case after case was reviewed. There were fifty of us in the class of senior students. Some were managing companies and were attending the class to be sure they were doing things the right way.

Time came for the final test. It was to cover the entire book and involved eighty cases that needed to be solved correctly. I stopped in the student lounge the day before the big test and found sample tests lying on the tables with the answers marked. I assumed that it was last year's test. Some students were taking notes. I looked at the testing style and realized that there would be multiple choice questions. The test looked very hard. I put the sample tests back on the table and returned to class. I studied until 2 a.m. to be prepared to do my best.

The day of the test everyone looked grim. The professor passed out the test that looked familiar. I went to work. Case one was difficult and I read all four solutions with great care. I marked the one that looked the most reasonable. I finished the first ten cases and I noted that some students were talking to the teacher. They turned in their papers and left the room. They must have quit and given up because the test was too hard. The rest of us students kept going forward until after the first hour there were only five us still at our desks. We were all the older students who wanted to get it right.

I finished in three hours and had only completed seventy of the cases. I got a "B" for the course. It was sad to note that there were forty-five students who got "A's," at least some of whom I felt could not be trusted.

Yard Work

One Saturday I started to clean out a spillway behind our new residence. We lived in a plush old neighborhood with a very large bay tree in our backyard. The house was on a hillside with several residences above us. When it rained, their water would run through our yard and down the driveway. The spillway was clogged and needed to be cleaned out. After several hours of work all that was left to do was to remove a small tree that was growing out of the drain that I tried to pull out by the roots. With one last mighty pull it came loose. I felt a pain in my shoulder but finished the cleanup. When I went in the house, I looked pale and exhausted from the hot work. I lay on the cool floor for a few minutes and got up. I had only a slight pain in my right leg.

During the night it got worse. I limped all the next day. My lower back began to hurt. I went to my classes and the office. After several days I went to the doctor, who put me on pain pills and asked me to come in for tests. The pain got so bad I couldn't drive. I spent a week in bed and could only crawl to the bathroom. When I finally got in for tests, which were extensive, they thought they would need to operate. After several more tests they determined that nothing could be done. They suggested that I try a chiropractor. One of my professors recommended a chiropractor who had helped him. I took his advice even though I had always equated them with witchdoctors.

The chiropractor took more x-rays and said he could see no problem. He began to give me treatments three days a week. I could walk as little, drive with a back support, and sleep through the night with pain pills. The pain would come and go. I carried a lumbar pillow wherever I went. I was learning to live with the pain.

A Box of Gold

One of the tasks that the director of the Adult Rehabilitation Center had asked me to do was to help price the collectables that came in off the trucks. The new employee determining prices called and asked me to check some items that had come in a whiskey box. She was sticking on five dollar tags, asked if I thought that was too much to ask. I took the box to my office and got out the pricing book for figurines.

What was this "Royal Dalton?" There were eighteen very old never out of the box figurines marked with early numbers. The books led us to believe that this was a salesperson's samples. They were all rare and very old with none of them priced less than $500. We priced them at a fraction of their value and put them on display at our number one store. They sold within a few days for a total of more than $1,500.

Christian Understanding Class.

There were over 150 men in the recovery program. I taught this Christian Understanding Class to all those who were interested in a full spiritual recovery. One young man came to all thirteen classes. He was a changed person, was doing very well and was a new happy worker. He came in one day with a troubled spirit wanting to know what he was doing wrong. He was black and looked a little like Michael Jordan. He described his problem.

It happened when he went out on the street and down by the bus stop where the drivers of the cars that pulled up waiting for the light to change would all click their door locks. I reminded him that God looked at the heart while man sees only our outward appearance.

New Leadership

Commissioner Andrew Miller was appointed as the National Commander. The new Territorial Commissioner James Osborne, let me know that the National Conference Center was not going to happen. I asked to be sent back to the Central Territory. He said he would work that move out. When I found out that we would be moving, I had called a friend who helped place officers and told him we wanted to come back north. He had an opening in the Kansas City area. Members of our family lived in the area so we were pleased with the move.

My back was still a problem. While I was helping to load the truck it went out again. Men from the center helped drive the truck to Nashville, while I rode in the back of a station wagon. Our son and his wife came and helped us get to our appointment. In a few days my back got better so I could walk.

CHAPTER SIXTEEN

GRANDVIEW, MISSOURI

We were assigned as the directors and corps officers for the almost new Booth Manor Corps and senior high-rise in Grandview, Missouri. There were eighty-five apartments, a public restaurant, offices, a chapel and a senior craft center. The three-room apartments had a bedroom, bath, living room and kitchen, and some apartments had two bedrooms. There was a year's waiting list to get in the center. It was a great place to serve. Many of the residents attended our Sunday services, and we helped make the center a happy place.

She Could Not Leave her House

One of our new residents had been rescued from her home by a family friend. Her husband had worked for the railroad and had purchased a lovely three-bedroom home in a quiet neighborhood of Kansas City. When he died, all she had was the home and a small pension. The neighborhood began to change slowly. Her good friends died or moved away. The block busters moved in and in several months there were "crack" houses down the block. Her yard was fenced in and she had to walk to a store several blocks away. When that store closed, she had to take the bus to shop. The crack users began to follow her down the street. She tried to sell her house but could find no buyers

She called welfare and they called us. We moved her to the front of the line. She moved in and for the first time in a long while, she said she had a good night's sleep. Her apartment rent with water and electric was $185 a month. She could eat a meal in our restaurant for three dollars. She attended our services and told us how she thanked God for this wonderful place.

Help with the Pain

Across the highway from our senior high-rise were the offices of a chiropractor who said he could help with my back pain. He had been a bandmaster of a local high school but felt the call to help others with their pain. He helped me some with a new procedure called the activator method. I could go for a week at a time without any help. He suggested that I began taking longer walks. I had a hard time standing and driving a car.

Our House

Our house, which was a five-spilt-level, was near our center. The basement, garage, first floor, second floor, and a loft all had five steps between floors. I set up my art equipment in the loft because the lighting was ideal. In the three years we were there I painted several paintings. Two of the Men's Social truck and horse-drawn wagon, both of which have been used as program covers. A painting of twin sisters was made from a small black and white photo taken during the depression era.

Our yard was full of flowers. One day we heard a soft rapping on our front door. When we opened it there was a small black girl who wanted to sell us some lovely flowers. We asked her where they had come from. She pointed to our flower bed. We thanked her and asked if she would like to keep them. She nodded and carried them across the street to her grandfather's home. They waved and we smiled back

The Childhood Home of Harry Truman

Harry lived in Grandview from 1906 to 1917 until he went off to the U.S. Army. The city was proud and held Harry Truman Days every summer.   We heard about Harry almost every day; someone said he was the only Democrat that they would like to see on Mount Rushmore. His retirement home and museum were nearby in Independence.

Off to the Holy Land

We were given an opportunity to join other officers on an eleven-day tour of the Holy Land.   My back, with the new treatments, was well enough to fly the twelve-hour flight to Austria, and the five hours to Israel as long as I could get up and walk around. We flew Air Jordan and landed in Amman, Jordan. We had two tour buses and traveled to sights mentioned in the *Bible*.

Our guide said that all Jordanians were either Amorites, Moabites or a mixture of the two. He believed they were the incestuous offspring of Lot's relationship with his daughters and proof of the existence of Sodom and Gomorrah. He also told us that one-third of the residents of Jordan were Christians and were left alone because they were willing to fight for their faith. We stood where Moses stood and looked at the Promised Land, where we could see the white gleaming buildings of Bethlehem forty miles across the Jordan valley.

We crossed the Jordan River at the Allen B. Bridge and drove the fifteen miles up the mountainside from Jericho to Jerusalem. We were taken to our hotel on the hills above the old city of Jerusalem. In the next few days we walked where Jesus, Paul, John, Moses, Daniel, David and many other *Bible* figures traveled. There was no time to fall asleep. We got on our buses at dawn and traveled until the sun went down, then in the evening spent our time walking the city streets.

I was able to take over five hundred pictures and record fifty hours of details given by our guide. I had remembered to bring extra film and batteries so when others went looking for batteries, we kept recording and taking pictures. When we returned home, we were able to present three different programs on the Holy Land.

Mother of the Year

Of the over fifty grandmothers in our center, about thirty attended our Sunday services. We announced that on Mother's Day we would be honoring one of our mothers with a special award. We checked around and found an outstanding lady who filled the bill. We sent out letters well in advance to the President, Governor, Mayor, Salvation Army General and many others asking them to send a word of encouragement to this lady to be placed in her book of memory. Family members were sent a note telling them of the date, informing them that we wanted this event to be a complete surprise. A family portrait would be taken of all the members who were present. We received letters from all those we had contacted.

On the day of the big event the family began to arrive early. They gathered in the dining room where their mother of the year could not see them. When we opened the doors of our chapel that held only sixty people, they came in. As there were seventy-five family members, we had to open the side doors. Some had come from California, others from hundreds of miles away. Our mother beamed with joy surrounded by the flowers they had brought.

We read the letters from family members who could not be there, and ended by reading the wonderful letter from the President of the United States. It was a great day for the mother and her family. The family thanked us and said they thought that they would have only been called to come to her funeral. We held this event in many of our corps appointments with a similar response.

Why South Bend, Indiana?

I shared with Headquarters that I was having a problem because so many of the older residents were dying. I felt like I was losing part of my family. They understood and we were farewelled to South Bend, Indiana, where we were responsible for the corps and the public relations for the seven corps in the area. We had served in this area before and knew of the many problems in the city.

Our new quarters were in a quiet part of the city, while the corps building was south and east of downtown near several houses of prostitution. The area south across the tracks was the center of the crack houses. Despite the surroundings we were a very busy place with fifty members from the area attending our services, a drop-in center for youth that was open weekdays, and about forty ladies in attendance at our two Home League meetings. In addition we provided space to GED classes for high school drop-outs weekday mornings. We were giving great service.

My back was hurting more and more each day. I called the offices of a Dr. Hunt and was told to come in the next day. He studied the x-rays and said he thought he knew what was really wrong. I discovered that he was the chiropractor for the Notre Dame sports' department and worked every day with pulled muscles. He said that in laymen's terms I had a shoulder blade pulled over a rib. Whatever he did, after eight treatments the pain of three years was gone. We both praised God and I knew why we were in South Bend.

We went in for our annual physicals and were questioned by our doctor about our diets. My blood count was irregular and revealed that I had a serious problem. He sent me to a blood clinic. After four or five visits they could not find the cause of the problem. As a last resort the doctor said they were going to treat me for pernicious anemia. After several weeks they said they caught it just in time. I later discovered that my mother and grandmother both were treated for this disease by eating raw liver. We both praised God and knew why we were sent to South Bend.

Evangelist in a Wheelchair

We shared the "Four Spiritual Laws" and conducted training class for their use with our members. An older couple who lived south on main street had taken part in the classes. She was in a wheelchair and went out in the early evening to speak to the girls who worked the streets in their area. In an eight-block area there would be as many as ten to fifteen girls on the street on weekends, one on every corner. Men came from miles away to be serviced by these girls. The police turned a blind eye most of the time. We were told that a girl who had been picked up by the police twice was moved by the mob to Gary, Detroit, or Toledo, because if they were picked up three times, they would be jailed for an extended period of time.

On this warm summer evening a new girl was on the corner. Our lady introduced herself and asked the young lady how old she was. She said she was fifteen and had come to town to meet a friend. When she got to the bus station, her friend was not there. A well-dressed lady said she could help and took her to her home. She was raped by an older black man and put out on the street to earn her room and board. They took away all of her regular clothing.

She was the daughter of a Baptist minister who lived near Toledo, Ohio. She told the Salvation Army grandmother that she had fought with her parents and run away from home. She thought they didn't want her back. Our worker told her to come to her house just down the street. She gave her something to eat and called her parents. They said, "Come home." We were away at camp so she called a friendly pastor who when told of the situation bought her a bus ticket and together they got her to the bus station. She never went back for her things. After several months and after the publication of this story the girls were moved off Main Street.

"I've Got AIDS"

A man, who came in for food every month, came in and said to our caseworker that he had contracted AIDS. He needed special food that cost fifty dollars a week. His parents and wife had put him out on the street, and he was living alone in a room without furniture. We said we would help. Several weeks later he came in for his food and said his wife had contracted AIDS and had moved in with him. In six months he died.

Christmas Basket Evangelism

We gave out over 1,500 food baskets at Christmas from a center away from our building each of the four years we were there. Each person who came in for their basket over the three days was given a Christmas song sheet, a white card and a bridge pencil and asked to put down name, address and church affiliation. We sent out letters and told the families when they should come in for their baskets. They were given numbers when they arrived and asked to sit in a waiting area while their baskets and toys were made ready.

We sang Christmas songs and shared a devotion which was based on the Four Laws. After the prayer we asked them to mark their white card with an "X" if they had prayed this prayer for the first time. If they had prayed a prayer like this before they should place an "O" behind their name. Many called later and thanked us for the food and toys, and told us of their renewed faith. Some said they were going back to their church.

Penny Saver Winner

The lady who delivered our weekly Penny Saver newspaper came by in an old van driven by her husband. She and her brother went door-to-door while the hound dogs barked out the van windows. She had no teeth, and in the winter she wore a ragged coat making us feel sorry for them.

We read in the paper that she had won the Indiana state lottery which at that time amounted to $1,500,000 in cash with all taxes paid. The state assigned a law firm to be sure that she would not lose her money. Three or four weeks passed and someone else delivered her papers. Then a new van drove down our street. They were back: the lady, the brother, her husband and the dogs. We asked what she had done with her winnings. She said she had bought the van and new linoleum for her kitchen. She was still buying lottery tickets

A Junior Soldier Killed in the War

We had about twenty-five children in our Junior Soldiers program. One of our best little seven-year-olds was sitting out in front of her house when gunfire broke out between the crack dealers down the street. A stray bullet killed the Junior Soldier as she sat on her front porch. The city fathers lost their patience and decided to take extreme measures. The crack dealers had been paying poor families up to one thousand dollars a day to use their houses. Many of the houses were owned by absentee landlords who would take no responsibility for their houses.

The city issued a notice in the paper that said all crack houses would be razed without notice. The city workers came with dump trucks, bulldozers and front-end loaders. They would shut off the gas, electric and water, then remove all appliances, plumbing and electrical fixtures, crush the building and load it unto the dump trucks. After that they would fill in the basement and cover it with black dirt. A crew would come and plant new sod, creating in one day an empty lot. Some square blocks had only three or four houses where there had been thirty homes. That part of town began to look like a city park. Apparently this system worked because the idea spread across the nation.

Lou Holtz

We had asked Lou Holtz, now a retired football coach, and sportscaster, author, and motivational speaker, to kick off our Christmas kettle appeal. Lou and the Notre Dame football team were then top national news. He was to come to our tree of lights in downtown South Bend on Friday at 11:45 a.m. The crowd was there and all four television stations were there to cover this event for the noon news. The band was playing old familiar Christmas carols. At 11:44 there was no Lou Holtz.

Suddenly from nowhere Lou Holts was standing beside me and asked, "What do we do now?" I told him to say whatever he wanted to say. He stepped to the mike, took out a check put it in the kettle and said kind words about the Army. He offered to answer several questions. The major networks moved in and he talked about football. We all sang, "Joy to the World," had a prayer for Christmas and thanked everyone for coming. Lou went on to serve on the Salvation Army National Advisory Board.

Moving on to Muskegon, Michigan

With four years to go before we retired the new Divisional Commander sent us to this fine family corps as an act of kindness. There were about sixty-five members in the corps who had been faithful over the years with no members of the corps on welfare. All the property had been taken care of and there was money in the bank.

17 Municipalities

Muskegon County was made up of seventeen city governments with separate police and fire departments. The police had a problem chasing lawbreakers as the officers could not cross over into someone else's area. While we were there, a Hot Pursuit law was passed that made it possible for the police to chase the lawbreakers.

With an area population of over 174,000 the criminals came from Detroit and other big cities to rob businesses along the highway. A jeweler just down the street from our building was robbed by five of Detroit's finest crooks who shot him several times. On their way out the door he shot the last man with a shotgun in the lower regions. When the jeweler recovered, the crooks tried to file a lawsuit against him.

Salvation Army Muskegon History

The word, "Muskegon," is derived from the Ottawa Indian term "Masquigon" meaning marshy river or swamp. Muskegon was once referred to as the Lumber Queen of the World because its rich collection of sawmills supplied the lumber to rebuild the Windy City after the Great Chicago Fire. During the lumbering era Muskegon boasted more millionaires than any other town in America and for a brief time had the highest per capita income in the United States.

The typical lumberman of the era was a young man in his twenties or thirties from New England, New York, or Pennsylvania who had enjoyed sufficient success in some previous occupation to build a small mill and to make a modest investment in Michigan timberlands. By the time the local lumber industry had reached its peak in the mid 1880s, forty-seven sawmills surrounded Muskegon Lake, while another sixteen dotted the shores of White Lake to the north. The top area industrialists included Newcomb McGraft, Charles Hackley, and Thomas Hume

What makes Hackley's story especially interesting is that he used much of his twelve million fortune to help his booming city of Muskegon meet the needs of a population that doubled during both the 1870s and 1880s.

Ladies from Canada

The Salvation Army invaded Muskegon, Michigan, in the 1880s, when two lassies from Windsor, Canada, opened fire. They established an Army that went to battle against sin wherever they could find it. This inland seaport was then the third largest city in Michigan. It was filled with hundreds of lumberjacks looking for excitement. The Salvation Army marched every evening from their hall to the blocks of bars and brothels in the downtown area. At the request of the bar owners the police stopped the marches and put the officers in jail. This happened more than ten times, each time being bailed out by an unknown benefactor.

Later it was discovered the Charles Hackley had paid their bail. He said the law should be changed to allow the Army to march. When the lumber mills began to close, the Army closed its corps. Later two corps were opened, one where members spoke English, and one where they spoke Swedish. The two were united in the 1940s. The Army has had a thriving ministry there for over one hundred years. When we arrived, we found an active corps with good community support and were allowed by law to conduct meetings anywhere we wished.

Jesus is a Way of L.I.F.E.

We carried on our usual spiritual programs with many activities, enrolled a number of new members, and had a small band that played Sunday morning and evening. Most of the soldiers had good jobs and gave great support. Many of the younger families had gone off to become Army officers.

Mr. Mustard at the Piano

This middle schoolteacher pulled up in front of our building in his very large Cadillac. He wanted to know if he could help with the Sunday Services. We needed a piano player, and he sat down at the baby grand and played several old familiar hymns. A collector of Jeep Wranglers with four-wheel drives, he lived with his brother on the edge of town in an ancient yellow mansion. He had five parked in his front yard. When we went to visit, we discovered that many of his rooms were filled with cages filled with pheasants that he would take to friendly farmers and release after hunting season was over. He had raised hundreds of birds at his own expense. He chose to teach in one of the poorest areas of the city and continued to help us all the years we were in Muskegon.

Off To The Holy Land Again!

We were given a chance to join a Holy Land study group for an eleven-day visit to Israel that planned to visit all the places we had missed on our first trip. Again we took pictures and recorded the guide's comments. Many of the places we had visited during our first visit were closed to visitors. Our group stopped in London for a day and toured the Salvation Army historical centers.

This was a refreshing time. We wished that this opportunity had been given to us thirty years earlier. One of the ways I used to remember each place was to pick up a rock and write on it the name of the location it was taken from. It is very effective to pass a rock around and talk about the walls of Jericho.

I Found A Job!

We had served over fifteen hundred families in December with baskets and toys leading many of them to first time decisions for Christ. More than four hundred people showed up for our Jesus

Birthday Party and Sunday morning worship service on Christmas Sunday.   Our chapel and basement youth hall were filled to overflowing. During the meeting I had suggested that if you were going to serve God, you should trust Him and not the state for your life support.

We received a call that one of our senior members had been taken to the hospital. We parked our car and went into the lobby. We were greeted by a well-dressed black lady. She asked if we remembered her. We tried to guess who she was. She said, "Last Christmas you told me if I wanted to live for God and if I could work, I should go find a job".   She said, "I found a job. I went to school and now I work in the hospital. I don't have to be on welfare any more."

Turkey is More Than a Country.

During our last year of active service it was brought to our attention that the Thanksgiving dinner that was provided for the poor in downtown Muskegon was attended by fewer people than the volunteers who came to help. They were going to shut down. What could we do to help?

We asked those coming in to sign up for Christmas baskets why they didn't go to the dinner. We were given many answers. "Our car wouldn't start." "We didn't have clean clothing." "The buses don't run on holidays." "We were sick." "They only want to take our picture." "The food was cold." "It was cold and we didn't have warm coats."

Our Advisory Board decided that we could do better. I suggested that we prepare the dinners and deliver them to the homes of the poor and shut-in. We began to take applications and a week before Thanksgiving we were up to 300 families. The sheriff, who was our Christmas chairman, agreed to work out the details. He was able to get a kitchen staff at a new high school to help prepare the dinners. We told the television stations that we needed drivers to help us deliver the dinners. We asked the public to donate pies and turkeys for the dinner. We received more than thirty turkeys, and almost two hundred pies.

We purchased all the other items. The addresses of the families were placed on cards and organized by areas. Those delivering the food would take no more than three or four cards and would need to drive to only one neighborhood. Families of three or more were given a pie. The others received a piece of pie for each family member. All meals were delivered hot and arrived within thirty minutes of their preparation. More than 1,500 meals were delivered by 2:00 p.m. with over twenty churches and 150 volunteers taking part.

CHAPTER SEVENTEEN

OUR RETIREMENT CAME

The little boy who was inspired by the man from God's Army on that long ago Christmas Eve, could never have imagined where the years would have taken him. What a wonderful day! With wife and family we celebrated our years of service. We had been asked to take the responsibility of Divisional Evangelists for the next three months until I reached the age of retirement.

We had decided to purchase a used motor home. An RV dealer in Grand Rapids, who with five other dealers was closed on Sundays so they and all their employees could go to church, said he liked to help returned missionaries. He sold us a four-year-old, 33' Winnebago Chieftain at his cost to be our temporary home in retirement. We lived in it while we did special meetings around Western Michigan.

Who Were Those Two Guys?

Headquarters called and said we were needed at the Western Michigan Holiness Conference in Ludington, Michigan, starting the next Sunday. The guest speaker had been taken ill and it was the Army's responsibility to provide the next speaker. I was to do eight nights of services for the seventeen Holiness churches that were taking part. I had the material for the Way of L.I.F.E. Seminar which I had been doing for the last twenty years.

On the first night over 250 people were present. A men's quartette provided music. I drew a black light picture each evening starting at 6:30 and displayed it during the time of offering and announcements. The hall was filled most nights by the time I started to draw.

For those members of the Holiness Movement who are reading

this story I give you this agenda. I spoke on the first evening about the "Uniqueness of Jesus" which brought everyone to focus on the source of our Holiness. All the other meetings fell in place: How to be sure you are a Christian, How to experience God's Love and Forgiveness, How to be filled with the Spirit, How to walk in the Spirit, How to Witness in the Spirit, How to share your Faith, and How to help fulfill the Great Commission.

After five days of the conference some of the leaders approached me and asked who I was. I told them I was from Divisional Headquarters in Grand Rapids. "No," they said, "Really who are you?" The last two speakers were from the national office. They were both very important. As they described them to me, I realize that they were Commissioners Andrew Miller and James Osborne while they were National Commanders. The week ended, and I realized that I had been standing in the shoes of two great men. The wife of one of the pastors, who had attended all the meetings, told me that she had been helped a great deal and had received some new life-changing inspiration for her ministry.

Retirement

We stayed on duty until I reached my 65th birthday. We settled with DHQ and started for Florida. We planned to stay in our motor home for the first year. We found an RV park in Zephyrhills, Florida, and settled in for the winter. With nowhere to put our Christmas tree we knew we needed a bigger place to live. The phone rang and Major David Atkins, our old friend from Little Rock, said the Adult Rehabilitation Center in Tampa had a house that we must buy. It was south of where we were living. We weren't sure, but we would look at it.

It was in a four-star adult mobile home park. As the house was what we were looking for, fully furnished, and priced in our range, we purchased it. We have lived in the Country Wood Park for our years in retirement. As part of the Lakeland Corps we are taking part in many of the corps activities.

How to Keep Sweet in Retirement

My sister Gladys had a friend who gave her a copy of what she called, "World Famous Fudge." My sister made sure that her family got a copy of it. I pass it on to you as the best fudge I have ever eaten.

<u>World Famous Fudge</u>

4 cups sugar   1-12 oz. semi-sweet chocolate chips
2 sticks butter 1-12 oz. German chocolate bar, chopped
1 cup milk   25 large marshmallows
1 tsp. vanilla   1 cup chopped nuts

Lightly butter a cookie sheet and set aside. In a large pot add milk, sugar, butter and vanilla. Bring to a rolling boil for 2 minutes. Remove from heat, add marshmallows and stir until smooth. Add both chocolates and stir until smooth. Add nuts and mix. Pour onto cookie sheet. Let cool, then refrigerate. (2 ½ lb.)

A Recipe for a Right Relationship with God

Dr. Bill Bright, founder of Campus Crusade for Christ, Inc., worked out a formula for a right relationship with God. I share this basic concept with you, excerpted from his book, *Have You Heard of the Four Spiritual Laws?* as I have had an opportunity to share with others over the years.

1. God loves you and offers a wonderful plan for your life.
2. Man is sinful and separated from God. Therefore, he cannot know and experience God's love and plan for his life.
3. Jesus Christ is God's only provision for man's sin. Through Him you can know and experience God's love and plan for your life.

4. We must individually receive Jesus Christ as Savior and Lord; then we can know and experience God's love and plan for our lives.

      You Can Receive Christ Right Now by Faith Through Prayer:

> *Lord Jesus, I need You. Thank You for dying on the cross for my sins. I open the door of my life and receive You as my Savior and Lord. Thank You for forgiving my sins and giving me eternal life. Take control of the throne of my life. Make me the kind of person You want me to be.*

This recipe can be shared with your friends.

Thank you for picking this book up. Take the book home. The fudge recipe is well worth the price of the book. Make the fudge before you read the book. It may take you two pans of fudge before you finish.

Also remember to give Jesus a try. He is better than the fudge.

#LKA